Wa
Fitness & Health thro

For Hartwig Gauder

Klaus Bös & Joachim Saam

WALKING

Fitness & Health
through Everyday Activity

Meyer & Meyer Sport

Original title: Tips für Walking
– Aachen : Meyer und Meyer Verlag, 1996
Translated by Jean Wanko

British Library Cataloguing in Publication Data
A catalogue record for this book is available from the British Library

Bös/Saam:
Walking – Fitness & Health through Everyday Activity/ Bös/Saam.
– Oxford : Meyer & Meyer Sport (UK) Ltd., 1999
ISBN 1-84126-001-0

© 1999 by Meyer & Meyer Sport (UK) Ltd
Oxford, Aachen, Olten (CH), Vienna, Québec, Lansing/ Michigan,
Adelaide, Auckland, Johannesburg
Internet: http://www.meyer-meyer-sports.com
e-mail: verlag@meyer-meyer-sports.com
Cover Photo: Polar Electro GmbH Deutschland, Büttelborn
List of photos and diagrams: see page 104-107
Cover design: Walter J. Neumann, N&N Design-Studio, Aachen
Cover and Type exposure: frw, Reiner Wahlen, Aachen
Typesetting: Quai
Editorial: Dr. Irmgard Jaeger, Aachen, John Cughlan
Printing: Burg Verlag Gastinger GmbH, Stolberg
Printed and bound in Germany
ISBN 1-84126-001-0

Contents

Contents

Introduction

Walking, as verified by scientific investigations and a wealth of experience, is a sporting activity which promotes good health and can be enjoyed by everyone. Walking is ideally suited to the demands of our modern, technical way of life in a civilized world, known only too well for its lack of movement.

Walking is a form of activity which does not presuppose any popular physical or mental skills, which can be integrated into any normal daily routine or leisure time regardless of age, and also demonstrates all the scientifically proven, health-enhancing features of endurance sports due to the minimal risk of injury.

This Walking book would like to offer leisure sportsmen and women, as well as the beginner, some tips for optimum and enjoyable health training through Walking.

Chapter 1 takes you into the topic area of Walking (as an endurance sport) and poses the question "How healthy is Walking?" Here you will discover the most important details of this sporting activity. What is Walking? Or: what effects does regular walking have on one's health? These sort of questions are dealt with quickly.

Chapter 2 helps you with your decision to start Walking. Using a simple health i.e. motivation-check, you can assess whether Walking is really the right sporting activity for you.

Finally in chapter 3 we get to the heart of the matter, which turns you into a Walking expert. In the middle of this third section you will find all the important aspects of Walking technique.

What sort of aids and means of support can be incorporated into Walking? These and other topics are addressed in chapter 4. Chapter 5 deals mainly with the basics of Walking training for preventative health reasons. This section holds the key to structuring your Walking training.

We have devoted chapter 6 to regulating your Walking training, so that with the aid of the Walking test you can assess your fitness and adjust to a Walking programme in line with your test result.

The Walking programmes for different levels of achievement and target groups are introduced and described in chapter 7. They are intended as an incentive towards specific training with Walking.

In chapters 8, 9 and 10, you will find specialised tips for areas like "Walking, as a Therapy", "Walking and Diet" and "Tips for the Expert".

Chapter 11 provides you with many practical tips by the professional Walker, Hartwig Gauder, Olympic medallist in Race-Walking.

And so, dear readers, with the following chapters, we have tried to present you with a book which is challenging, yet easy to read. Diagrams and photos should help you to understand the most important information quickly and effortlessly.

Klaus Bös/Joachim Saam

1   Walking – a Healthy Kind of Sport

Walking is described as a "gently healthy kind of sport". That sounds very abstract. What indeed is health? And why is Walking readily described as a healthy sport?

1.1   What is Walking?

The word "Walking" comes from America and means "to go on foot". However Walking is more than merely going along on foot, as we normally understand it in our daily lives. The simplest way to describe Walking is a kind of fast, sportive moving along on foot. There are innumerable variations on this theme: Walking can be comfortable or brisk, meditative and relaxing, can be carried out at full power or even with additional weights.

However, you should not confuse Walking with the competitive sport "Race-Walking", where one aims for the highest levels of performance in accordance with international standards. Walking, on the other hand, is fun, fitness, health and it is individuality which counts. One's own personal achievement and goals are of prime importance.

Walking technique is very simple and resembles fast marching with a more sporting look. The extreme hip rotations, by which competitive Race-Walkers try to achieve brief contact with the ground and thereby increase their speed, are avoided during Walking.

1.2   Walking, Endurance Sport and Health

Health is a constantly changing process. Our language refers to health in the singular. Yet medicine in the meantime knows about more than 60,000 illnesses! However, even today no satisfactory definition has been discovered for the term "health". Are there maybe several kinds of health?

Traditionally medicine refers to health as the absence of disease. But would you describe a sportsman, at the peak of his achievement, who has become the world's best at his sport, as "ill" because of chronic knee injuries? Or is it right to describe young people as "ill" when they can neither manage comparable physical performance nor seem particularly resilient?

The best way to approach the phenomenon of health is from a holistic point of view. A human being is a complete unit of body, mind and spirit, and this ancient way of looking at humanity is advocated by the World Health Organisation (WHO). The WHO defines health as an ideal objective as follows: "Health is not just the absence of illness, but a state of complete physical, mental and social well-being" (WHO 1987).

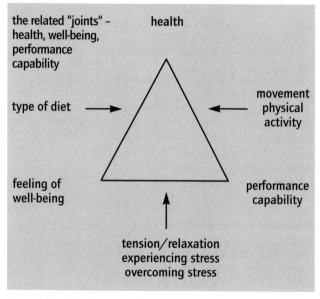

Diagram 1: Correlation of movement, diet and relaxation

Endurance sport, especially Walking has, alongside one's attitude to diet and stress assimilation, a scientifically proven influence on our health. The marked characteristics of Walking are physical and emotional well-being, physical and mental capacity for work (fitness), and health in a holistic context.

By means of Walking, wholefoods diet and active relaxation (summed up simply as protective health factors under your control), you can improve and maintain your performance capability throughout your life in a very simple way.

1.3   The Effects of Walking on Your Health

The ability to maintain a high level of performance is just as important in our everyday life as in a sporting context. Endurance, alongside strength, speed and co-ordination (mobility, agility) are important, but also as a cornerstone comes the ability to maintain a certain amount of stress over a long period of time. This is not only useful in sporting achievements but also helps one to have a concentrated and relaxed approach to the completion of everyday tasks e.g. at work.

However, the risks of some extreme endurance sports have hitherto been overlooked e.g. no research had been done into the effects on one's brain and immune system. It has now been proved that extreme endurance training can lead to loss of memory and weakening of one's immune system, let alone the damage and wear and tear caused to an athlete's joints and bones.

The medical and sporting world have been in no doubt about the beneficial effects of Walking for a long time. One should use up between 1,000 and 2,000 calories per kilo a week in order to prevent heart disease. Alongside Walking the traditional endurance sports such as swimming, cross-country skiing, cycling and running are to be recommended.

When compared with the traditional endurance sports, Walking has the great advantage that one can achieve healthy results for body, mind and spirit with comparable less effort and exertion and more or less without injury. To put it precisely – looking after yourself – *Walking, the gentle health sport.*

1.3.1   The Effects of Walking on one's Mobility System

Leg and posterior muscles are strengthened by walking and muscle tone is improved, which increases one's resilience to ligament and joint injuries. In addition to that, all the trunk muscles (back, pelvis, stomach) are brought into action, which is good for an upright spine. Also by strengthening one's thigh muscles there is less strain on knee and hip joints.

Bones gain increased stability by Walking. The correct balance of re-building and degeneration of bones is maintained for much longer than if there were little or no movement. For example, a frequent problem of ageing, osteoporosis, can be effectively prevented, but one should also keep to a calcium-rich diet for extra support, as brittle bones and the build up of kyphosis in the spine (hunchback) can be prevented. Cartilage, tendons and ligaments become stronger, more elastic and less breakable.

A TIP:

As a beginner, or with long breaks in between times, you can achieve quick results from Walking. But please note that the adaptability of your muscles to performance is considerably faster than your passive mobility system i.e. your tendons, ligaments, cartilage and bones need 2/3 as long a time to increase their dimension and flexibility. So, increase your speed and length of Walking very carefully. If joints start to hurt this indicates overloading, and you should reduce or stop your training immediately.

1.3.2   The Effects of Walking on one's Heart and Circulatory System

Your level of endurance in performance is primarily dependent on the ability of your heart and circulatory system to regulate and adapt (heart muscle, body and the lungs' vascular system) and your metabolic system (dietary exchange between blood vessels and muscle cells).

How much could you achieve without a heart trained for minimal endurance? Your heart and circulatory system would pack up when faced with the slightest exertion like walking or climbing stairs. So there is a direct correlation between the heart's capacity to work and endurance capacity. The more endurance-trained you are, the more economically can your heart cope with the same amount of physical exertion (i.e. it has less of a problem with larger loads by beating less often).

A trained sportsperson – be it in health, leisure or performance sport, has a greater capacity to resist tiredness when practising sport. In health circles high regard is given to one's endurance capacity, because this in turn has a positive influence on one's heart and circulatory system, metabolism and blood flow through the body's organs. Many diseases of our wealthy society e.g. coronary heart disease, high blood pressure, or imbalance of body fats and sugars, could be avoided. Scientific research has shown that controlled endurance sport affords a certain amount of protection against these diseases.

Some unavoidable and frequently occurring stress situations can be compensated for much better if your heart is well-trained to cope, and thus you can achieve much more.

The Salutogenic Model of Health – dynamic balance between risk factors and protection factors

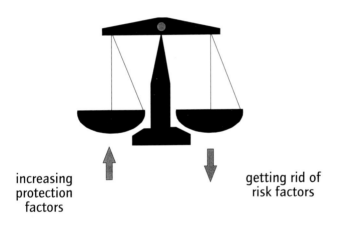

increasing protection factors

getting rid of risk factors

Diagram 2: Balance of protection to risk faktors

So far, endurance training, including Walking, can be seen as an important preventative measure against movement deficiencies and in rehabilitation programmes.

If we now turn our attention to necessary adjustment features for endurance training, then we need to differentiate between aerobic and anaerobic availability of energy. In health sport circles one is primarily interested in aerobic endurance performance with its capacity to protect. This can only be carried out by the muscles when suitably balanced with energy i.e. that the supply of oxygen fits in with expended energy (steady state). The body will only fall back on its own fat supplies during aerobic concentration of energy and that over a long time span.

When the muscles begin to work one's metabolism quadruples the rate of its resting position.

Consequently a larger amount of oxygen is needed which is released through the increased blood flow (rise in heartbeat frequency and volume of blood through the heart).

Normally one's heart and circulatory system can supply a muscle with as much oxygen as it needs to acquire energy. The resulting adaptability of the heart and circulatory system, and thereby the measurable effects of endurance sport, are an increase in the size of one's heart (economising by reducing the frequency of heartbeat but simultaneously increasing the volume flow per beat) and, in addition to that, an improvement in the supplies to the muscles due to capillary action (extension of blood-carrying capillaries and opening up of non blood-carrying capillaries).

1. Improvement in one's ability to absorb oxygen
2. Improvement in one's capacity to transport oxygen
3. Reduction of heartbeat frequency
4. Increase of the stroke volume of the heart
5. Improvement of blood flow in the heart muscle by the formation of tiny branches
6. Increased heart muscle size
7. Improvement in the heart muscles' capacity to contract
8. Improved blood supply to the heart
9. Reduction of peripheral capillary opposition
10. Lowering of the diastolic blood pressure

Diagram 3: The ten most important effects of Walking on heart and circulatory system

Anaerobic training – that is very intensive, short-term exertion e.g. sprinting – is of little significance to health sport. The supply of oxygen to the muscles is inadequate during anaerobic exertion, the whole organism suffers a shortage of oxygen and acquires energy without burning oxygen. The result is a build-up of lactic acid and an over-acidification of the muscle.

The build-up of lactic acid contains a considerable health risk. The product lactose, part of the metabolic waste process, is not only disposed of in the liver through using up oxygen, but during intense exertion also in the heart muscle.

It is at this point that a previously undetected, damaged heart muscle can (e.g. through a narrowing or closed artery) run the risk of insufficient oxygen due to the additional necessary amount of oxygen for disposing of lactic acid.

A further risk for a heart neither trained for nor used to intense exertion is the outbreak of possible cholesterol deposits in the arteries around the heart. These deposits can suddenly get into the capillaries and lead to a blood clot: the start of a heart attack!

Thus many a leisure athlete runs the risk of sudden death from a heart attack just because of his bursts of intense activity.

So, in conclusion, let's grasp hold of the following: – the less one's heart beats during the same constant output, the better one's endurance ability during output, and also the better your "Motor" or heart muscle's blood supply, and the better its supply of oxygen during a similarly economised pattern of working.

If we look at it another way, the athlete trained in endurance sport performs better than the untrained athlete although heartbeat frequency is the same. The lower heartbeat frequency is directly related to the hearts' size, namely the volume of blood it has to pump.

1.3.3   The Effects of Walking on the Risk Factors in Heart and Circulation Disorders

Arteriosclerosis
Arteriosclerosis (a gradual narrowing in diameter of the artery) can be prevented by Walking. It has been proved that the composition of and concentration of blood fats (as a direct cause of narrowing of the arteries) in the blood is changed, in fact reduced by Walking. Because the flow and flowing speed of the blood are increased, the risk of

further deposits on the artery walls, and at the same time the progressive sclerosis of the arteries, are reduced.

High blood pressure

Manifest high blood pressure is a measurable disease syndrome which increases the risk of suffering from a dangerous heart-circulatory illness. The main cause of high blood pressure is often overweight. Through insufficient movement and the vast range of choice, often out of all proportion in our consumer society, an unfavourable ratio occurs between calorie intake and calorie consumption. More calories are absorbed than the necessary daily need.

It has been proved that Walking can help you to lose weight, depending on how often, how long for, and the intensity of movement. In addition, regular Walking has a favourable effect on a permanent lowering of blood pressure levels.

1.3.4   The Effects of Walking on one's Metabolism

The internal combustion motors in the body are the so-called mitochondria, innate in every body cell and responsible for the energy supply to this tiniest unit of the organism. In the muscular cell compound (muscle fibre in muscle bundles to the muscle), the centres of energy generate the muscle movements by a complicated biochemical process.

It depends on the amount of physical exertion and endurance potential as to whether more or less mitochondria are in the muscle cells.

A well-trained endurance athlete shows considerably more mitochondria in the muscles which carry the highest load than a less-trained athlete.

Whilst oxygen is being used glucose molecules are broken up with the aid of a complex enzyme unit within the mitochondrium and energy-rich phosphate compounds (adenosine triphosphate) are made available. These phosphate compounds react during the use of calcium with the smallest, mobile contraction units in the muscles, which are made out of protein cells, and then the muscle fibres contract. If there is sufficient movement stimulus (electric nerve impulse) across the nerve-muscle unit, then a number of these contraction systems contract and move one of the body's extremities (e.g. the arm) by pulling a tendon.

At the beginning of any physical activity energy spent is first dissolved in the blood, before all the other energy deposits present in the body (glycogen, fats, proteins) are prevailed upon. The greater the movement stimulus the more muscle cells are activated, and so the enzyme activity is increased and thus the greater the consumption of energy and the degration of bodily-energy resources. Metabolic waste products, of which the best-known is carbon-dioxide, are exuded via cell membranes into the blood-flow and then disposed of. Carbon-dioxide, for example, is breathed out through the lungs.

If the concentration of carbon-dioxide in the blood increases, then this stimulates the respiratory system to take more oxygen into the lungs by deeper breaths. In order to transport a larger amount of oxygen faster to the working muscles during physical exercise, the heart as an "engine pump" needs to carry more blood by increasing its beating rate or increasing the blood flow.

1. Increase of the mitochondria
2. Improvement of the muscles' enzyme activity
3. Increase in haemoglobin content in the muscle cells (and therefore oxygen supply)
4. Increase of intra-muscular energising substances (glycogen, triglycerides, energy-rich phosphates)
5. Change in the cholesterol composition by an improved ratio of
6. Increase in the amount of High Density Lipoproteins by simultaneous reduction of Low Density Lipoproteins.
7. Increase in the glucose level
8. Reduction of acid level in the urine
9. Improvement in bone compound

Diagram 4: The nine most important effects of Walking on one's metabolism

Just like one's metabolism the heart and circulatory system adapt to regular exercise, as already described. The heart muscle expands and gets fatter, becomes stronger and can subsequently pump more blood per discharge out of its muscle into the body's extremities.

Simultaneously, the amount of blood per beat is increased. The Myoglobin content in the blood is raised and sees to it that all the organs in the body get a better oxygen supply. (Myoglobin is a protein, which combines with oxygen to carry it in the blood).

Having read this considerably shortened description of a complicated biochemical process imagine yourself permanently raising your metabolic rate to a higher level, even if you take breaks occasionally. Your metabolic balance is simply raised and you do not acquire bits of "flab" so quickly ...

1.3.5   Combating Everyday Stress by Walking

Walking compensates the daily stress factors of modern-day living. Tension, irritation, nervousness, impatience, hectic behaviour, anger, bad temper, getting worked up, fear and much more besides, which send our vegetative nervous system into physical reactions beyond our control like: dizziness, breathing problems, racing heartbeat, headache, are all evidently influenced and even got rid of by a release of so-called anti-stress hormones unique to one's body during Walking.

Further sociological and psychological studies indicate that Walkers have a greater feeling of self-esteem, or are more self-assured when compared with non-sporting people.

Walking can increase one's feeling of well-being, strengthen one's confidence as well as prevent anxiety and can help to get rid of depression.

1. Increase in feeling of well-being
2. Reduction of states of anxiety and depression
3. Increase in one's feeling of self-esteem
4. Establishing confidence in oneself
5. Improvement in overcoming stress
6. Improved awareness and concentration

Diagram 5: The six most important effects of Walking on one's psyche

Because Walking takes place in the countryside, you have to "switch off". Enjoying nature is top priority. So, when selecting suitable routes, you should choose ones where noise, exhaust fumes etc. cannot disturb or impede you.

You will find that all demands made on you, both at work and in private, can be tackled in an easier and more relaxed way.

2   Health-Check for Walking

Did you know that Walking is **the** type of endurance sport by which you can stay i.e. become fit and healthy, with minimum effort? Walking puts demands on your body in such a way that it is mainly accumulated amounts of one's own body fat which are got rid of. This is because energy for Walking is mainly released by using up body fats through gentle and careful exertion of medium intensity spread out over a lengthy period of time. Moreover, Walking is conducted at as low an intensity as possible but high enough to ensure always that the muscle energy processes have enough oxygen. Using the following example and a simple health-check afterwards, you can check whether Walking is the correct and necessary sporting activity for you, or whether, when you are ill or otherwise handicapped health-wise, Walking could conceivably be a risk to you.

By means of a very simple sports-medical example we should first like to clarify what happens inside the body when you set off Walking, i.e. the physiological effect of Walking.

Assume you are relaxed and then start Walking. After about three seconds the fast deliverer of energy to the muscles, **adenosine triphosphate**, and after ten seconds, **creatine phosphate** have been used up and must constantly be replaced at high speed. These phosphates, you see, are the substances which immediately release muscle movement by a chemical-physical reaction in the muscle cells.

Your body must deliver a new supply straight away, otherwise there is no more muscle movement. So the body produces new adenosine triphosphate fast in a fraction of a second. To do this, it first works on sugars released into the blood in the mitochondrium (s. p. 18), then sugar products (glycogen) stored in the muscle cells. Untrained athletes use up these suppliers after about 30 minutes and trained athletes after a maximum of 45 minutes.

So, after about ten seconds of beginning to walk, sugar combustion has reached its peak. Starting at the same time, and running parallel to it, is fat combustion, the so-called glycolysis. The contribution of both metabolic activities to the delivery of the energy process is constantly changing. To begin with it seems as if only sugar combustion is delivering the necessary energy for Walking, but after about 45 minutes it is mainly (70%) fat combustion.

The fat deposits in the body are subsequently got rid of.

Imagine now that you go Walking every day. Amounts of fat are transformed into muscle. Tissue becomes more taut, parts of the body take on a better shape. You will not necessarily be any lighter, but the relationship of fat to amount of muscle will change in favour of the energy-needing muscle structure and will thus also do your health good. You will find other healthy effects of Walking in chapter 1.

Now, with the aid of a few simple questions, see if Walking is a suitable sportive type of movement for you. You will notice that there is hardly anyone who cannot simply go out and walk.

2.1   Risk Check

There are one or two people with certain notable ailments (called "people at risk"), who should take advice before going out Walking. You could be one of those at risk if you answer any of the following questions with "Yes". Therefore, it is a good idea to first check with your own G.P. whether gentle Walking could be a health risk to you. Please confirm by means of a small "Risk Check" whether you have ever detected the following symptoms, or even if they occur regularly.

Do you have any rhythmic or uneven disturbance to your heart?	Yes O	No O
Have you any pain in your joints?	Yes O	No O
Were you in hospital at all last year?	Yes O	No O
Have you a cold or temperature at the moment?	Yes O	No O

Diagram 6: Check list for risks

If you have answered "Yes" to any of these questions, you must consult your doctor as to whether Walking is the right kind of movement for you.

- In the case of heart problems a load-tolerance ECG (electro-cardiogram) should be carried out. By such a test, irregularities in heart function can be established and risks weighed up.

- The causes of joint and muscle pain must also be looked into by a doctor. It is possible that arthritic or rheumatic complaints can be the cause of the problem, but it is also possible to eradicate them by movement: "He who rests, rusts" as the wise saying goes!

- It is not a good idea to go Walking with a high temperature (over 100°F or 38°C) or with a respiratory infection, cough or cold, as this could lead to pneumonia or an inflammation of the heart muscle. These risks should not be underestimated and are to be avoided. Get rid of your cold or temperature first.

2.2   When You Should Walk

We would now like to take our eyes off illnesses and all sorts of risks. Looked at positively the following people should certainly start Walking straight away, as long as none of the previous questions has been answered with "Yes".

Walking is the ideal sporting activity for people who:

- sit longer than nine hours per day
- stand longer than nine hours per day
- move about in the fresh air less than 15 minutes per day
- climb less than 25 stairs per day
- do less than 30 minutes sport per week
- get out of breath when walking fast or climbing stairs
- get pains in their joints after sitting or lying down
- feel tension in the back, neck and shoulders
- have an accelerated pulse rate at rest (of more than 80 beats per minute.)
- are overweight.

Diagram 7: Motivation list

If you fit into one or more of the above categories it is high time you got moving! If you do not, you will get one of the ailments directly related to lack of movement with its negative symptoms.

2.3   When You Certainly Should Not Walk

Unfortunately there are some people, suffering from the following ailments, who should certainly not walk:

- When suffering severe circulatory problems accompanied by pain in the affected limbs when resting.
- If you cannot walk further than 100 metres without sensing pain in your legs.
- When angina pectoris is unstable i.e. if you have any new and variable pain in your chest when resting which extends down the left-hand side of your body, accompanied by shortage of breath. This could mark the beginning of a heart attack.
- With obvious hypertension i.e. high blood pressure constantly more than 140 to 90 mmHg.
- When suffering a severe irregular heartbeat, accompanied by shortage of breath and tightness in one's chest.
- If you have acute coronary artery stenosis i.e. advanced narrowing of the arteries around the heart.

Diagram 8: Criteria for exclusion from Walking

If in any doubt you should seek a doctor's advice before any complications arise. For men and women over the age of 35, you can ask for a comprehensive health check-up at one of the Well-Man or Well-Women clinics.

Photo 1: Body posture

3   WALKING TECHNIQUE

Walking technique is different from normal walking. But also normal walking is by no means the same from person to person. Everyone develops their own individual style of walking during the course of their life, and experienced body therapists could find out a lot about the state of an individual's physical and mental state by observing these various styles of walking, which are often a barometer of mood and how one is feeling.

A lowered head, upper part of the body bent over studying one's shoes and small, careful steps indicate a depressive and fearful person, who has got the "weight of the world on his shoulders". On the other hand, someone who steps out with head held up high and chest out, indicates an active, optimistic person, who happily looks ahead into the future.

Take note of how you walk and observe others. Also try and describe your current mood by observing your body and you may discover some interesting things about yourself.

3.1   Body Posture during Walking

The upper part of the body is held erect. Look ahead, your gaze must not be permanently fixed on the ground. Put your shoulders back and lift your chest, and thus, you will avoid tension in the muscles of your shoulder, neck and back when you walk.

Start by mastering step and foot movement. Walk a few steps to begin with and then greater distances. Increase your speed more than you would in normal walking.

3.2   Rolling Your Feet and Stepping Technique

Put your feet down in such a way that your toes are pointing the way you want to go.

Slight outward or inward-positioning of the feet is quite normal. Set your feet down in an exaggerated way heel first with each step, and then consciously roll your foot along the complete sole/outer edge down towards the toes, until you press off the ground powerfully with your toes.

Photo 2: Stepping technique

3.3   Active Support from the Arms

Now involve your arms actively in the whole movement. Like a pendulum you can swing them loosely in harmonious teamwork with your feet. The range of arm movement is considerable: take your arms rhythmically from your hips up to your shoulders, holding your hands loosely closed or slightly open. Clenched fists indicate rigidity or tension.

3.4   Walking Speed, Frequency and Duration

Speed, frequency and duration of one's steps each influence the other. If you increase your Walking speed then the frequency also increases and at the same time the length of step decreases. However, the reverse applies when you try to take much bigger steps in order to cover a greater area with less steps, then the frequency of steps is reduced. One's own individual optimum lies somewhere between these components, which you must discover yourself. Normally, this optimum sorts itself out when you Walk longer distances.

Photo 3: Arm movement

Photo 4: Walking – total movement

Count your step frequency from time to time. Our experience is that you should reach a step frequency of 110-130 steps per minute depending on your level of training.

3.5   Breathing Technique

Has it ever occurred to you when studying the anatomical picture of a lung that it resembles a gigantic tree root? Just like a tree, the lungs inside our body undertake the vital process of breathing, which we can see reflected in nature for millions of years and which we cannot escape from as living components in the cycle of nature.

The lung branches off into millions of little twiglets, so-called alveoli, and only recognisable under the microscope. That is where the exchange of oxygen into the blood takes place. From every heartbeat the blood absorbs oxygen from the lung and transports it to other organs of the body where it is used up.

The resulting waste product, carbon-dioxide, is taken back to the lungs by the returning blood in the veins and then breathed out.

When we walk we stimulate our breathing organs to inhale more air into the lungs. The amount of oxygen we manage to take in depends on the size of our heart, lungs, and the capacity of our blood for transporting such an amount of oxygen. This is in turn dependent on the ability of the muscles to absorb the oxygen and use it. It is possible to train all of these components.

By means of the simple exertion "Walking", normal breathing, which we do without thinking, becomes faster. Depth of breathing becomes shallower, because the body has to absorb more oxygen. Thus, untrained people get out of breath more quickly than those well-trained. If unaccustomed, intense, physical exertion takes place like a lengthy sprint to catch a bus, the muscular ability to absorb oxygen and use it up is insufficient, so that an imbalance occurs. Oxygen is exhaled again without being used. The muscles work without oxygen, leading to their over-acidity, and the performance potential of the body decreases rapidly. If you get out of breath whilst Walking this indicates too great a speed.

You can support your breathing process by consciously inhaling deeply and evenly to the rhythm of your Walking steps. Breathe through your nose, and then the air, warmed-up moistened and cleaned in this way, reaches the upper lung, the bronchia.

A TIP:

Try a rhythm of breathing just right for you, only you will know if it is right. Normally your breathing will adapt quite naturally to the exertions of Walking. For example, breathe in for three steps and then out during the next three. If you still run out of breath, this indicates that you are Walking too fast and run the risk of over-acidifying your muscles. The increased need of oxygen must then be compensated by breathing through your mouth. Reduce your Walking speed slowly until you stop. Now we would recommend your not only breathing through your mouth, but simultaneously through your nose, ensuring that exhaling generally takes longer than inhaling.

4 Equipment

"There is no such thing as bad weather, merely the wrong clothes ..." as the saying goes and which is highly appropriate to the outdoor sport of Walking. Only when it is really raining "cats and dogs", or if extremes in temperature, or high ozone levels are recorded, then you should manage without your Walking. Walking is the kind of sport which needs no particular kind of equipment in order to practise it. For example, if you can only Walk during your lunch break or to and from work, then we would recommend that you wear more casual clothes, in which you can move about freely and feel good. Light cotton garments are an advantage here. For everyday Walking many sorts of shoes are all right with the exception of high-heeled shoes. For sportive Walking you need shoes, which have an air-cushioned sole.

4.1 Clothing

If you intend practising sportive Walking over a long period of time, then you must buy comfortable sports or leisure clothing i.e. track suits, so that nothing hinders or confines your Walking style. Moreover, you will discover that if the fabric of your sports clothing is easy-care and easily washable, you will find that it makes you sweat considerably during your Walking.

If it is cool weather we would recommend that you wear one or two thin sweatshirts over your T-shirt, and only take a thick jacket with you in extreme weather conditions. Do not ever forget that your skin is a breathing organ and therefore a lined or padded jacket is only suited to bitterly cold weather or icy winds, otherwise you will find it an unpleasant hindrance. Sweatshirts, however, you can tie round your hips to cope with a sudden change in temperature.

The thousand and one available types of rain capes and jackets enable you to Walk in all weathers, regardless of whether it is raining or stormy. Fabrics which can "breathe" are best suited to the purpose, and which are not only waterproof from the outside, but can also let out sweat in the form of steam as this brings beneficial cooling to the skin. These sorts of jackets are nevertheless somewhat more expensive than simple rain or wind jackets.

4.2   Shoes

It is important to pay special attention to one's shoes because the soles of one's feet and ankles are put under particular strain during sportive Walking. For this reason jogging and running shoes are especially suitable for Walking. The excellent air-cushioning qualities of the soles, and their light and flexible structure, are particularly good for Walking on a hard surface such as asphalt.

Another advantage of such sport shoes is that they can be washed in the washing machine up to 40°C provided that they are not made all of leather.

For the more performance-orientated Walker we would recommend buying special "Walking" shoes.

You will discover that the heel-end of such a shoe is at an angle, so that the heel has maximum support during the constant setting down movement of the foot, and thereby minimising the rolling-on movement of the feet. Pushing off from the ground is strengthened by means of a slight elevation of the sole under the ball of the foot, ensuring that you really catapult away like an athlete off his starting block.

TIPS:

1. Buy shoes which are well-padded or cushioned. This can definitely prevent or minimise joint and ligament problems.
2. Do not buy shoes which are too small. Walking shoes should normally be a size bigger than everyday shoes so that you do not get blisters, and your feet have enough room to move.
3. Check with a doctor or foot specialist what sort of tread you have and ask to be shown the appropriate shoes. You can correct slight turns of the foot outwards or inwards by wearing special shoes.
4. If you already have any aches and pains in your joints you should first let a doctor diagnose the cause. Sometimes a shoe-inlay can ameliorate or reduce the difficulties.

4.3   Accessories

It is possible to buy teaching and music cassettes for Walking. These are available for various levels of ability from beginner to power-walker.

You can use the rhythmical pieces of music in a variety of different ways. Varying speeds allow you to Walk faster or slower, or you can sail into a certain mood. Of course, if you want to and have the necessary skills, you can develop your own music programmes. However, you should bear in mind your training goal and speed of Walking when you choose the music tempo. Fast music motivates us to fast Walking, slower music to more relaxed and might be called meditative Walking.

A few other items of equipment usefully enable you to Walk at any time of year and in all weathers i.e. in the summer, a sun hat, sunglasses or a sweatband as protection against ultra-violet rays and heat. In the winter, hats, scarves and gloves help you to defy wind and cold.

4.4   Training Aids

As well as **Walkmans** for playing music cassettes, you can also get **rubber bands** (with practice posters) with build-up exercises to complete the equipment of your Walking hours.

Something else which is really great is a new, modern, wrist-size **measuring instrument**, whereby Walking fanatics can measure their pulse rate or heartbeat. These are the real trendies, who fit the spirit of the age of our information-technological society! You can control your pulse rate considerably with such a piece of equipment. The frequency of your heartbeat can constantly be made visible (even during Walking) on a watch (receiver and measuring station) by means of a chest strap (transmitter).

Such measuring equipment works by means of a microcomputer, which can store pulse rate data for a whole hour's Walking. This data can be recalled later and you can thus effectively check whether you have been Walking at the speed which is right for you. With this apparatus you are ideally equipped for planning and checking your Walking.

Some people undoubtedly regard the heartbeat measuring apparatus as an interesting toy, but we think it is essential when recovering from a coronary heart disease. The apparatus works exactly like an ECG, you can hardly feel it and it serves as an early warning system for possible further complications.

For anyone interested in Walking from the beginner to the real expert, an attractive and motivating **video** has been produced with the help of Hartwig Gauder, Olympic medallist in Sportive Walking and now also an enthusiastic Walker. It is called **"Walking – Schnelle Schritte zu einer gesunden Lebensweise"** (Walking – Qick steps towards a Healthy Way of Living) and helps you both to start Walking and guides your training.

In the appendix you will find **addresses** from which you can obtain the heartbeat frequency apparatus or the video, and you will also find further **reading tips.**

When selecting further walking equipment you should give your own imagination free reign. When Walking in the U.S.A. was still in its infancy and a small group of fans tried out their first "Walks", one Walked almost "naked" i.e. without any special equipment.

Now, particularly keen fitness Walkers carry little dumb-bells in their hands so that they can train their upper part of the body, or carry special Walking rucksacks in order to stimulate their training. We do not want to limit you in any way; try out anything for a laugh – go on!

Shoes	Clothing	Accessories	Training Devices
Walking shoes ❑	Tracksuit ❑	Sun protection ❑	Puls rate apparatus ❑
well-padded sports shoes ❑	Jogging suit ❑	Music cassettes ❑	Rubber band ❑
	Rainwear ❑	Walkman ❑	Dumb-bells ❑
		Sweatbands ❑	Walking rucksack ❑
			Video ❑

Diagram 9: Checklist of basic equipment

4.5   Choice of Terrain

Parks with large areas of grass and big leafy trees or high hedges and light woodlands are ideal for Walking. Alternatively, footpaths across the fields through lines of trees. This is where you will find rest and relaxation most quickly. The natural environment awakens all our senses: the air fans your skin; hedges, meadows and woods invite you to be adventurous.

A TIP:

Listen to all the different leaf-rustling sounds and how many different ways birds can twitter as you Walk along rhythmically and lightly as if on wings! Feel in your innermost being how the air flows through your body, giving you renewed energy. Open up your soul and your spirit and become one with your environment, and you will find that Walking becomes an unforgettable experience!

4.6   The Ground

It is important to Walk on even, firm ground, so that you avoid constant changes in rhythm and tempo. So, look for firm paths, because if you are constantly looking out for uneven ground, you will find it much harder to switch off and let go of everyday problems. Gravel or stony paths or loose sandy paths are all unsuitable because of the risk of injury.

The best sort of paths are well-kept soft and springy woodland paths, like one finds in evergreen woods or autumnal paths covered with a thin layer of dry leaves. We can also warmly recommend firm sand, such as you can find at the seaside. Then you should Walk barefoot, enjoying the pleasantly gentle foot massage free of charge!

Photo 5: Type of terrain and ground

All one's bodily functions are influenced by internal and external reactions, so that our senses and feelings sometimes play a trick on us.

For example we often do not notice that we are overloading our body because it does not report back, or because we have not learnt to tune in to it properly. Therefore it is better to be guided by both objective measurements as well as subjective feelings when out Walking. Of course it is all right to set out Walking just when you feel like it and fun should be paramount.

However, you should note a few basics of load control with which you can optimise your Walking training (without minimising your enjoyment). These should help you with minimal time taken up to achieve the maximum level of health efficiency.

Your training will never become boring if you vary the load level, the length of your route or the Walking speed.

5.1   Heart Rate and Walking Speed

When at rest the heart beats approximately between five and seven litres of blood through one's veins and arteries by pumping 60 to 80 times per minute depending on age, sex, constitution and state of fitness.

According to the amount of exertion, i.e. intensity of Walking, the heart rate can increase to over 200 beats per minute. The current heart rate tells us something about the actual level of physical exertion.

Scientists have already discovered through much research into sports medicine with which heartbeat frequencies it is safe to train in endurance sport areas which have a positive effect on one's health. These depend on one's age, and there are also weight and sex deviations from these data.

However, a few simple **rules** of thumb have stood the test of time, which have been put together in the following table:

Age	Normal preservation of heart rate 180 - old age	Heart rate during training 200 - old age	220 - old age maximum heart rate
20	160	180	200
25	155	175	195
30	150	170	190
35	145	165	185
40	140	160	180
45	135	155	175
50	130	150	170
55	125	145	165
60	120	140	160
65	115	135	155
70	110	130	150

Diagram 10: Health-effective heartbeat frequencies

Maximum heart rate:

During an appropriate test the maximum heart rate should not exceed a limit of 220 beats/minute minus one's age. So, this means 170 beats/minute for a 50 year-old person. This maximum pulse rate should only be reached by well-trained people or under expert guidance.

Heart rate during training:

The optimum heart rate during training is around 200 beats/minute minus one's age, but you need to be well in training for such a pulse rate. This means 150 beats/minutes for a 50 year-old person.

Normal preservation of heart rate:

The heart rate during training should reach at least 180 beats/minute minus one's age and this means 130 beats /minute for a 50 year-old person. This rule of thumb (Trimming 130) is also called "Baum'sche Regel".

There are also more complicated formulae for ascertaining one's training pulse rate, according to which beginners and senior citizens should have around 60-70% of the maximum pulse rate, but well-trained people around 70-80%.

It is easy to measure your heart rate and this is also the best way to find your individual Walking tempo. If you Walk at a steady pace at the level of your heart rate during training, that is your correct Walking tempo.

You will certainly suddenly notice during the course of regular training that you can Walk faster, but your training heart rate remains the same.

Those are the first obviously physical effects of training towards improved performance which we have described above.

5.1.1   Measuring Heart Rate

It is virtually impossible to measure heart rate whilst Walking unless you possess an electronic heart rate measuring instrument.

So, you must measure it by your pulse rate, as both are usually the same in healthy people. However, the pulse rate in one's extremities e.g. when measured at the wrist, can sometimes deviate from one's heart rate and be higher or lower i.e. with certain illnesses.

People who are known to have such deviations should use a heartbeat measuring instrument in order to avoid over-straining their heart.

For most people, however, measuring one's pulse rate is perfectly adequate and you should proceed as follows:

- Before you set off Walking you should have practised measuring your pulse rate several times. If you are out of breath and your pulse rate is very fast it is not easy to find it let alone measure it.
- To check your pulse rate during Walking training you need to stand still, and to take your pulse, you need a watch with second hand.
- Take your pulse on the lower arm, at the main artery leading to the hand above the wrist. Practise applying slight pressure with index, middle or ring finger at the point between the tendons and the bone. Can you feel your pulse?
- When you have found your pulse, look at your watch and count the beats for 15 seconds. Multiply this number by four and you have got your present training pulse rate per minute.

Photo 6: Taking one's pulse

One's pulse rate is influenced in a few other ways i.e. by medicines, infections, having a temperature, or by climatic conditions and the weather which can raise or lower it.

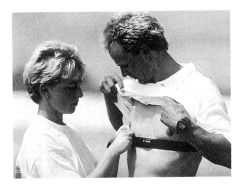

Photo 7: Taking one's pulse electronically

As well as Walking in line with your pulse rate, you must pay attention to your own body signals. Sometimes, one is not as fit as one ought to be. If your sense of well-being was good both during and after Walking, your breathing slow, deep and even, you had no joint or muscle problems and your training pulse rate was more or less in line with the standard rule of thumb, then you were at one with yourself. Each time you go out you must find out your ideal Walking tempo for yourself.

A TIP:

Measuring your pulse rate manually takes a lot of practice and is often unreliable. If you want accurate information about your training pulse it is worth investing in an electronic measuring instrument. For high-risk people, or with a history of coronary heart disease, an accurate ECG reading is indispensable.

5.2   Intensity and Duration

During the first 4-5 weeks after starting your Walking training, if you have not been involved in any appreciable amount of physical or sporting activities for years, it is advisable to do 30 minutes Walking once a week keeping an eye on your pulse rate. Once you have completed this phase of getting used to and building up your Walking, you can then Walk twice a week with a recommended gap of two days in between each session. In this way you will both gently increase and stabilise your fitness. You should not think of increasing your amount of training to three or four sessions per week until you have completed six months of regular Walking.

You must slowly adapt the duration of Walking per training session to your level of fitness. After about twelve weeks you can increase your length of training to 45 minutes per session and then after six months to 60 minutes.

If you build up your training slowly and constantly the performance level you have attained will remain stable for much longer than if you have bumped it up to a high level too quickly. The body is very good at registering what we do to it, and it will be grateful for a gentle and careful increase in performance.

5.3   Training Frequency

The sports scientists discovered, starting with the effect on one's health and, on average, well-trained Walkers, that one should complete a maximum amount of Walking training three to four times a week lasting between 45 and 60 minutes with a training pulse rate in line with one's age. When dividing up your week it is important to leave enough time for regeneration in between each training session. The reason for this is that the adaptational reactions for the body's health take place in between one's Walking hours.

Training frequency and duration each week depends on how fit you are at the time. To enjoy the gentle adjustment stimuli of Walking to the full, you must know how much you can expect of yourself.

Your actual level of output and health at the time is where you start, and you can establish your physical condition by means of the simple Walking test, which you will find in chapter 6.3.

5.4   Warming-up

It is dangerous to compare the human body to a machine as this suggests that the living body can be taken to a workshop and collected after a while when repaired. This is the point at which there is a dividing line between bio-systems and a machine. One can exchange parts of a machine, but we have got our body all our life! The body is the foundation, the unique and irreparable resource, the well from which we draw our strength.

Your body needs to be warmed-up for higher levels of output, otherwise premature seizing up will occur, just like an engine. Therefore, you should approach each session of Walking training slowly with an appropriate warming-up programme.

Warming-up starts in one's head, and you need to prepare yourself mentally for the Walking training ahead. Gather your thoughts together and concentrate on the exercise. Warm-up in yourself the feeling of being on your own, and become more aware of your body with each exercise as you feel and think your way into yourself.

5.4.1   The Little Multiplication Table for Warming-up

Certain muscles, depending on how they are made, their bodily function and the strain they are subjected to, are inclined to become permanently shorter if not used.

These muscles become shorter, and their ability to stretch and move properly becomes limited. The important factor in warming-up these muscles is to stretch them.

Warming-up is by no means a nuisance factor. You can feel how the most important muscles and groups of muscles are slowly and carefully stretched and limbered up. Whilst warming-up you will soon discover the principle of stretching, with proper relaxation following afterwards.

5.4.2   Stretching

When a muscle is stretched, the movable, interwoven muscle structures are pulled apart and passive elements like tendons and ligaments are stretched. This makes the muscle more mobile and flexible.

Tendons and ligaments, with which the muscles are connected to the skeleton, and which, by muscle power, pass movement onto the bones, adapt to regular stretching of the muscle and become more elastic without losing their breaking power. If you do simple stretching exercises regularly you can prevent injuries like strained muscles during your Walking training. Longer term the elasticity of the joints is not only maintained but improved.

Stretch your muscles as follows:

- Feel your way into the slow stretching movements. Keep on breathing quietly and deeply, avoiding strained breathing (do not hold your breath).
- Stretch your muscles slowly, until you sense a pleasant pulling, and avoid any jerky or rocking movements.
- Stretch your muscles for between eight to twelve seconds and then slowly relax.
- Finally, limber up your muscles by careful shaking and rocking, or by gentle tapping and stroking with your hands.

Warm-up each time you go training in the order of exercises given (see warming-up programme – chapter 7.1).

Begin your warming-up session by Walking some 100 metres at a comfortable speed in order to get your circulation going and to stimulate the flow of blood and warmth throughout all the muscles. Stretching your muscles will then be considerably easier and pleasanter.

5.5   A Personal Training Programme

If each day begins with your not being able to look at yourself each morning in the mirror, and you get the feeling that a stranger is looking at you, then the saying is true that the day is far spent before it has even begun. If you are a grumpy old thing in the mornings and you say "That is not me, is it?" then it is high time you did something to improve your image.

What do you think: is this really your inescapable destiny? Or could you decide that each day becomes a pearl, which you can string one by one onto your own, life-long, personal string of pearls? Of course, we are not always free to choose and sometimes have to complete unpleasant tasks. But you do not need to let yourself be got down by so many external events, and you are the architect of your own good fortune, as the saying goes. Undertake something you enjoy each day, something which is a real pleasure to do and which makes you feel good. Spoil yourself and see things which come your way in a calm and composed manner. Plan your events for the day to include moments of relaxation, ensuring you do something which is good fun. Thus each day will become a blob of cream for your personal happiness.

All the stress which has accumulated during the day can be shaken off best and fastest in the evening by going Walking. But, you must give yourself time for this, because if you try and fit this in between appointments, you will create more stress for yourself through lack of time.

Walking will become pleasant relaxation for you as a result of the gentle exertion in the fresh air. Stale office air will be exchanged quickly for air full of oxygen filling your lungs. Your organs will be well and truly showered with oxygen.

Your agitated nerves will receive a welcome massage which really does them good. All the tightened blood vessels ready to ring alarm bells expand, and other organs of the body, previously working at their uttermost limit, are tenderly relaxed. A pleasantly heavy warmth spreads through your body, other circulating thoughts and problems vanish from your consciousness and you leave the day behind you.

Your spirit begins to flow and you sense yourself drawing on new strength. Let your soul sway gently: and what sporting activity lends itself better to this than Walking?

5.6   The Weather and Walking

Let the sun and air get to your skin during the summer and it will be grateful. However, you must protect yourself from dangerous ultra-violet rays, and for this purpose suntan creams with a light protection factor are indispensible.

You should certainly not Walk in the burning midday sun. The cooler times of day in the morning or the late evening are ideal, not the least because of the reduced amounts of ozone. Ozone is unfortunately around in large amounts in the summer.

Ozone near the ground is an irritant gas and arises from the reaction of sulphurous substances with the sun's rays (main culprits are cars and *industry). This is the reason for such high levels of ozone in recent years, especially in the summer. Ozone causes breathing difficulties for many people, and they should avoid Walking on days when ozone levels are high. However, if you can only arrange your Walking around the middle of the day, when the ozone levels are high, you should avoid busy roads.*

Finally, Walkers surely do not dig their own graves, do they? Whenever you can, do not use your car. Then you will really get into Walking and the environment has a welcome breathing space.

JOACHIM SAAM

MONDAY, 10TH FEBRUARY 1997

	MONDAY	TUESDAY	WEDNESDAY	THURSDAY	FRIDAY
8:00				Walking	
8:30	(University) Sport Conference				
9:00					
9:30					
10:00					
10:30					
11:00		Lectures	Tutorial		
11:30					
12:00					
12:30					
13:00	Lunch with Huber				
13:30					
14:00					Walking
14:30					
15:00	Exam Heinzelmann				
15:30					
16:00				Hairdresser	
other:	18:00-19:30 Walking		18:00-19:30 Walking	16:30-18:00 Hairdresser	

Diagram 11: Engagements for the week/ Walking

JOACHIM SAAM
EVENTS ON MONDAY, 10TH FEBRUARY 1997

Mon.	Tues.	Wed.	Th.	Fr.	Sat.	Sun.
					1	2
3	4	5	6	7	8	9
10	11	12	13	14	15	16
17	18	19	20	21	22	23
24	25	26	27	28		

Printed on Sunday 9th February 1997 at 19.43

8:00		Other engagements:
8:30	(University) Sport Conference	18:00-18:30 Walking (Meeting point at the lake)
9:00		
9:30		
10:00		
10:30		
11:00		
11:30		
12:.00		Tasks (Active):
12:.30		
13:00	Lunch with Huber	
13:30		
14:00		
14:30		
15:00	Exam – Heinzelmann	
15:30		
16:00		

Diagram 11: Engagements for the week/Walking

To Walk and training your Walking – is there any difference? We are of the opinion – yes. On the one hand you can throw yourself headlong into Walking training whenever you feel like it and simply set off at your whim. It is virtually impossible to over exert yourself. But you can also direct your Walking training objectively with the aid of well-tested training measures. Just like a ship's captain can more or less steer towards the horizon by following his nose and perchance will reach his destination (or run aground!?); he can also navigate by the stars or by means of a compass. What we are trying to say is that you can so plan your training that you are neither over or understretched. The following sections reveal how you can achieve this.

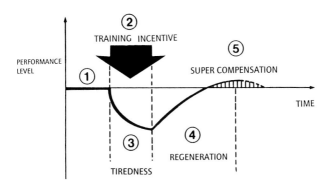

The principle of biological adjustment: starting with the individual's level of performance

(1) during the training incentive (2) tiredness (3) is reached after about two hours of training with a falling of the performance level. At the end of the training session, a regeneration or recovery period (4) begins lasting variable amounts of time depending on the amount of exertion previously. During the final regeneration period a higher level of performance is reached than at the outset: super compensation (5). If no further training exertion takes place, there is a gradual return to the starting level.

Diagram 12: Super compensation

6.1   Stress and Regeneration

After an hour's walking your body is normally pleasantly tired and its efficiency less than at the outset. It wants to compensate this tiredness in order to reach its peak again (compensation). But in order to do this it naturally needs plenty of time, depending on the level of tiredness. Super-compensation is the name given to this performance-increasing adjustment procedure after an exhausting period of training.

The body instinctively sees to it that extra reserves of energy are released and stored, as a precaution, so to speak against further strain, and these energy reserves enable the body to perform even better than before (super or over-compensation). The body's efficiency is thus greater than at the outset of training.

This principle of super compensation is drawn on to the uttermost limit of the achievable by high-performance athletes. Health-sportsmen and women like Walkers are concerned with reaching their individual best and then maintaining it.

The rule of thumb for this is: **begin gently, increase slowly, maintain your pattern.** If you have regard for the principle of super compensation, allow sufficient recovery time and renew your training at the right time with a stress level appropriate to your age, then there is no danger of overloading your body. Your body will send out certain signals in time when too much is expected of it.

6.2.   The Body's Warning Signals

The following signs of over exertion, or increasing intensity of training too fast, are muscle and/or joint pains, muscle stiffness, tiredness and feeling worn out. It is almost impossible to overexert oneself when Walking but, should it happen, here are some ideas as to what to do:

- If muscle or joint pains occur during Walking you should defer or stop Walking altogether.
- Acute pain can be alleviated by cooling the affected joint (e.g. with an ice pack).
- Recurrent muscle spasms or pain should be treated with warmth (warm shower, hot cushion, infra-red light). If in doubt , consult your doctor for advice.

- Muscles soreness is not serious, but is nevertheless a painful injury for the muscle where minute tears have occurred in the muscle fibres. The symptoms have usually disappeared after two days. If muscles soreness occurs after Walking, wait until it is completely better before you Walk again. You should not massage stiff legs but stroking the surface with slight pressure from the hands and a bit of warmth are permitted.

- Tiredness and feeling worn out can indicate overtraining, when you have not given your body enough time to regenerate itself. If you repeatedly start walking again when your body is in a state of exhaustion, your body cannot compensate for the loss of energy, let alone super compensate. In time this leads to a decline in performance which manifests itself in an aversion (to Walking) and a feeling of limpness. If this happens you should stop your Walking training and renew your energy. Give your body time for regeneration.

The same principles apply to the Walking beginner or the sports beginner as to the more performance-orientated Walkers. There is a saying that "strength lies in stillness". Take it to heart, because you are not trying to win any prizes with your Walking.

6.3   The 2 km Walking Test (UKK – Walk – Test)

In the next section we would like to introduce you to a way in which you can regulate your Walking training i.e. a **Walking test,** which has been developed and scientifically tested for health and leisure sport by Dr. Pekka Oja and Dr. Raija Laukkannen (UKK Institute in Tampere, Finland) in collaboration with Prof. Klaus Bös (Walking Institute Germany).

   Using this method of testing you can check your physical health and performance condition and thus maintain the correct levels for organising your Walking training further.

The Walking test belongs to scientifically proven endurance test procedures, by means of which you can estimate your maximum capacity for oxygen absorption (VO_2 max). The maximum capacity for oxygen absorption is the gross criterion for endurance performance ability. You can determine your general fitness level with the Walking test, attach yourself to a prescribed Walking programme or plan your own training.

The long-term documentation of test data permits statements about an individual course of performance.

Before you start, you must complete a risk check (page 23, diagram 6).

This is an absolute "must" for people who have not done any regular sport for more than two years. If in any doubt, ask your doctor beforehand.

Photo 8: Walking test situation

Sender

Surname, christian name

House nr. and road

Town and post code

Telephone

Please include a cheque for £ 11.60/DM 30,-. You will receive as soon as possible a computer evaluation of your Walking test results with a personal Walking training programme. Evaluation for groups (for more than ten test cards) £ 5.80/DM 15,-.

IDAG

Walking Institut
Badstraße 52

D 76669 Bad Schoenborn

Diagram 13: Walking test-card

Test-card for the Walking Test

Before you do the WALKING test, please answer the following questions:

1. Have you any heart disease or high blood pressure?   Yes ( )   No ( )
2. Have you any blocked arteries?   Yes ( )   No ( )
3. Have you been ill or injured recently?   Yes ( )   No ( )
4. Are you ill at the moment or do you feel unwell?   Yes ( )   No ( )
5. Are you taking medicine for reducing your heart rate e.g. beta blockers?   Yes ( )   No ( )

If you have answered any of these questions with "Yes", you should consult a doctor before doing the Walking test.

Do you do sport?   No ( )   Yes, up to 2 hours per week ( )   Yes, more than 2 hours per week ( )

If "Yes". What kind of sport do you do?   WALKING ( )

Another endurance sport (e.g. jogging, running)   ( )

Another kind of sport (e.g.: tennis, soccer , judo etc.)   ( )

_____

As a result of your WALKING training, do you want to   IMPROVE ( )   or **MAINTAIN** ( ) your performance potential?

_____

What is your favourite method of training?   **With another person?** ( )   On your own? ( )

_____

Personal details: **Test results after 2,000 metres:**

Sex (f./m): _____   Height (in centimetres or feet and inches): _____   Walking time _____ (minutes) _____ seconds

Age (in years): _____   Weight (in kilos or stones and pounds): _____   Load on pulse _____ (count per minute)

We advise the over-70s not to do the Walking test.

For this age-group, we have devised a special Walking programme (see chapter 7.5). If you would still like to check your performance potential by doing the Walking test, please ask your doctor's advice first.

For completing and evaluating the Walking test we have prepared two methods for you:

1.	Testing and evaluating yourself

Complete the test yourself using the following instructions. You will then receive a simplified test evaluation and an initial estimation of your fitness, which you can then co-ordinate with the given training programmes.

2.	Test evaluation by professionals using a computer

Complete the Walking test as prescribed either on your own or with guidance, fill in your results on the prepared card, and send it to:

Walking-Institut
"Stichwort Walking-Test"
Badstraße 52
D 76669 Bad Schoenborn

You can also get further information from the UKK Institute, Kaupinpuistonkatu 1, SF 33500 Tampere.

In return for a small fee to cover costs, you will receive a **computerised evaluation** of your test data with the results of **your physical performance potential** as well as tips and suggestions for your **own personal Walking training**. Return postal charges are also included in the fee.

Now you can follow the instructions for completion of your Walking test and both evaluations are carried out in the same way.

Please note that you will only receive adequate results and correct interpretation of your physical performance potential if you adhere strictly to the instructions. If not, you may have to repeat the Walking test.

6.3.1 Preparations

Before you do the Walking test, you need to prepare yourself carefully:

Measuring instruments

You will need a watch with second-hand or better still, a stopwatch, because you need to measure your Walking time in minutes and seconds. Also, at the end, you must measure your test pulse rate (pulse beats per minute).

You will find this described on page 41, and ideally you need an electronic pulse-measuring instrument. Take a notepad and pencil with you for writing down your test-time pulse.

Choosing your test route

Look for even, flat ground and mark out your start. Measure off about 2,000 metres (ideally using a bike with kilometre counter). It would be easier to find a sports ground with a 400 metre track and then all you need to do is complete five circuits.

Warming-up

Prior to your Walking test you should warm-up. Walk 200-300 metres and see how fast you can Walk without getting out of breath. This will give you a feeling for the right Walking speed as you do the test.

6.3.2 Performance

Start

Note your starting time in minutes and seconds. Walk as fast as you can without over exerting yourself, as it is important that you feel good whilst carrying out the test. Try and maintain this speed throughout the course without any spurt at the end.

If you sense any shortage of breath, reduce your speed. This means you are Walking too fast, your pulse rate increases and can falsify the test result.

Aim

2,000 metres can indeed be a long way. When you reach the finishing line note your completion time in minutes and seconds, and then concentrate on measuring your pulse rate. Take your pulse at your wrist, look at your watch and count your pulse beats for 15 seconds.

Write the result on your notepad and multiply it by four to get the rate per minute. It is easy to take the wrong reading when you are out of breath.

You have just been mainly exerting your body to see what it is capable of and now we need your head to evaluate your Walking test performance.

You can read off your endurance test result from the following chart which will help you evaluate it.

6.3.3   Evaluation

In order for you to read off your test result easily from the following chart many thousands of healthy men and women of all ages have willingly completed the Walking test and undergone sports medical tests. So you are not the first!

Walking Test time			
Men		**Women**	
age	average **Walking time** minutes:seconds	age	average **Walking time** minutes:seconds
20	13:45 – 15:15	20	15:45 – 17:15
25	14:00 – 15:30	25	15:52 – 17:22
30	14:15 – 15:45	30	16:00 – 17:30
35	14:30 – 16:00	35	16:07 – 17:37
40	14:45 – 16:15	40	16:15 – 17:45
45	15:00 – 16:30	45	16:22 – 17:52
50	16:15 – 16:45	50	16:30 – 18:00
55	15:30 – 17:00	55	16:37 – 18:07
60	15:45 – 17:15	60	16:45 – 18:15
65	16:15 – 17:45	65	17:00 – 18:30
70	16:45 – 18:15	70	17:15 – 18:45

Diagram 14: Chart of Walking test times

| My Walking time: | Min: | | Sec. | | Ø | ☐ | < Ø | ☐ | > Ø | ☐ |

Walking time

Proceed as follows: Find your age-group in the Walking test chart. Average Walking times are given for each age-group. Is your Walking time average, below or above average?

Pulse rate

In order to evaluate your test result it is not enough just to look at the Walking time, but you must also examine this in relation to your pulse rate. Your pulse rate is the real guideline for evaluating your Walking test performance.

When doing the Walking test you should fully exert yourself and reach a test pulse rate of around 80-85% of the heart's greatest potential. Return to your age-group on the chart and see whether your test pulse rate is within the desired range, or whether it is higher or lower.

age	Test pulse rate 80-85% max.pulse (s/min)
20	160 – 190
25	156 – 185
30	152 – 181
35	148 – 176
40	144 – 171
45	140 – 166
50	136 – 162
55	132 – 157
60	128 – 152
65	124 – 147
70	120 – 143

Diagram 15: Pulse rates when under stress during men's and women's Walking tests

| My stress pulse rate: | | s/min: | | Ø | ☐ | < Ø | ☐ | > Ø | ☐ |

Evaluation of the Walking test

Fitness level	Result	Evaluation	Recommendation	See page
1	My test pulse rate and Walking test time are above average (pulse rate low, test time fast).	You are extremely fit! Your endurance performance potential is excellent.	Walking programme for experts	77
2	My test pulse rate is too high but my Walking test time is above average (test pulse higher than average, test time fast).	Your level of fitness is still good, but you possibly overdid it a bit during the test. On no account should you Walk with such a high pulse rate.	Walking programme for advanced people	75
3	My test pulse rate is low, but my Walking test time is only average (test pulse – low, test-time – medium).	Your endurance level is satisfactory, but maybe you did not start fast enough or you did not exert yourself sufficiently. A tip from us: Repeat the Walking test.	Walking programme for advanced people	75
4	My test pulse rate is a bit high and my Walking test time below average (test pulse – high, test time – slow).	You have undoubtedly exerted yourself a lot, but your result is unsatisfactory. Set to work on your fat (i.e. fight the flab!) This is no reason to bury your head in the sand. Walking is ideal for you and the best way to do something for yourself.	Walking programme for beginners	73

Diagram 16: Evaluation of the Walking test

7   Walking Programmes

The following Walking programmes have been worked out to correspond with the test results. Thus they contain tips for optimum pulse rates during training, length of training for one individual Walking training session, and the frequency of training sessions per week; all of this is to fit in with your current achieving and performance ability and your age.

Apart from the test result all Walkers should warm-up prior to their Walking training, and so we are starting with your warming-up programme, bearing in mind the muscles and muscle groups primarily used in Walking.

7.1   Warming-up Programme

First Walk a distance of about 500 metres, choosing a moderate speed. Increase your speed for 250 metres, reaching your maximum speed by the end of the course. Then complete the following exercises in the order in which they are given.

If some of them are new to you carry them out carefully following the instructions, so that you feel your way into the stretching movement and the pull from stretching. The warming-up programme takes about 15-20 minutes to complete each exercise.

Exercise 1   **Stretching the calf muscles**

- Do a slight fall forwards, supporting yourself with both arms. One leg remains stretched out behind you (see diagram 26).
- Now push your pelvis forwards trying not to give up stretching your leg behind you.
- See that your whole foot remains in touch with the floor. You must not lift your heel.
- Repeat the exercise for the other leg.
- You are doing this exercise properly if you feel a pulling in your upper calves.

Exercise	Muscle/Muscle group	Exercise goal	Repeat times
1	Little and big calf muscles	Stretching	3
2	Calf muscle group/achilles tendon	Stretching	2
3	Rear thigh muscles	Stretching	3
4	Rear thigh muscles and calf muscles	Stretching	1
5	Hip-bending muscles	Stretching	3
6	Front thigh muscles	Stretching	3
7	Inner thigh muscles	Stretching	2
8	Side trunk muscles	Stretching	2
9	Chest muscles	Stretching	3
10	Side neck-bending muscles	Stretching	3

Diagram 17: A summary of the demands made on muscle groups during Walking

Photo 9: Stretching the calf muscles

Exercise 2   ### Stretching the calf muscles (supplementing exercise 1)

- Start at the same point as for exercise 1. The difference lies in how you carry out the exercise, as you will undoubtedly see.

- Now bend your back leg (unlike the first exercise) and your front leg bends with it (see diagram 27). Your pelvis pushes down gently and your foot remains flat on the ground.
- You should feel a pulling sensation whilst stretching, both in your achilles tendon but also in your lower calf. Repeat the exercise with your other leg.

Photo 10: Stretching the calf muscles (supplementing exercise 1)

Exercise 3   **Stretching the rear thigh muscles**

- Cross your legs, keeping them straight whilst standing up, so that both feet have their outer edges next to each other.
- Bend your trunk forward, but keep your back straight. Support yourself with both hands on the front of your thigh. Your legs remain stretched out (see diagram 28).
- Only bend until you get a pulling sensation from the stretching at the back of your thigh and in your knee joint.
- Repeat the exercise for the other leg.
- It is important that you keep your back in the prescribed position during this exercise. Check with your hands placed on the crucial points whether you can maintain this position. As soon as you sense that the lumbar vertebrae no longer provides a hollow for your hand i.e. your chest touches the other hand, then the rear

thigh muscle can be stretched no further.

- Any further trunk movement is cheating and will be determined by the mobility of the lumbar vertebrae. In certain cases the ligaments in this area are loosened, which increases reciprocal sliding about of the vertebrae and also the danger of wear and tear on the inter-vertebral discs.

Photo 11: Stretching the rear thigh muscles

Exercise 4   **Stretching the rear thigh muscles and calf muscles (supplementing exercise 3)**

- This exercise merely augments the third warming-up exercise. The stretching principle should be reinforced because the rear thigh muscles and calf muscles constitute a so-called chain of muscles. For this reason a shortened calf muscle group, which is connected to the rear thigh muscles by tendons and ligaments, can easily cause problems at the base of the spine. By stretching both muscle groups thoroughly you can improve the stretchability of the whole muscle chain.
- Complete the exercise as described for exercise 3. You will reinforce the incentive to stretch by setting your stretched-out front leg on its heel and pulling your toes towards you.
- Can you feel an increased pull on your joint as you stretch? Be careful not to give way with your trunk and thus avoid moving.

Photo 12: Stretching the rear muscles and calf muscles

Exercise 5	**Stretching the hip-bending muscles**

- Take a big step forward, bigger than your normal stride (see diagram 30). One's weight rests on the back leg from the knee downwards and the front leg is bent at a right angle.
- The trunk is in line with the back leg. Push your hip as far as it will go downwards towards the floor.
- Repeat the exercise for the other leg.
- You are doing the exercise correctly if you feel a pulling in your loins when you stretch, and also on the inside of your thighs.

Photo 13: Stretching the hip-bending muscles

Exercise 6	**Stretching the front thigh muscles**

- Stand in an upright position avoiding a big hollow in the small of your back as you strain your tummy and bottom muscles. Your pelvis remains steady and you can stretch your thigh muscles without affecting any other group of muscles or putting unnecessary strain on your lumbar vertebrae.
- Now with your hand pull your heel up to your bottom. Guide your

knee slowly backwards until you feel a pulling sensation at the front of your thigh. Avoid a hollow in the small of your back by simultaneously pushing your pelvis forward.
- Repeat the exercise for your other leg.

Photo 14: Stretching the front thigh muscles

Exercise 7	**Stretching the side thigh muscles**

- Take a big step to the side (see diagram 32). The trunk remains upright with your feet pointing forwards.
- Put all your weight on one leg as you bend your knee slightly, but no further than a right angle at the knee joint. The other leg remains stretched out.
- Stay in this position. Can you feel a pulling on the inside thigh of your stretched out leg as you stretch? You can increase the stretching by tilting your trunk slowly and carefully sideways in the direction of the stretched-out leg.

Photo 15: Stretching the side thigh muscles

Exercise 8	**Stretching the side trunk muscles and mobilising the lumbar vertebrae**

- Stand with your legs slightly apart (see diagram 33) and both arms straight out down the outside of your legs.
- Reach out over your head with your left arm and bend to the right,

during which your right arm moves down your outside leg. Try at the same time to reach as far as possible to the right with your left arm.

- Repeat the exercise for the other side.
- Please note: do not bend forwards. Your pelvis should not leave the upright position.

Photo 16: Stretching the side trunk muscles and mobilising the lumbar vertebrae

- Again stand with your legs slightly apart. Touch the back of your neck (behind your ears), so that you can keep your upper arms horizontal and out to the sides level with your shoulders.
- Now move your arms slowly backwards without letting go of your neck. If you are doing the exercise correctly you should feel a pull on your chest muscles as you stretch.
- Be careful that you do not get a hollow in the small of your back as you stretch tummy and bottom muscles, and keep your pelvis fixed.

Photo 17: Stretching the chest muscles

Exercise 10   **Stretching the side neck-bending muscles**

- Stand upright in a relaxed position with your feet apart in line with your shoulders and looking straight ahead.
- Reach out over your head towards your ear and pull your head gently sideways.
- Now pull the opposite shoulder towards the ground until you feel a pull on the nape of your neck as you stretch.

Photo 18: Stretching the side neck-bending muscles

After warming-up you can start your Walking programme which you have worked out for yourself from your test results.

The following table will help you to see quickly, at a glance, the best training pulse rate for deciding each individual Walking programme.

age	Maximum pulse	Training pulse rate			
	100%	60%	75%	80%	90%
20	200	120	150	160	180
25	195	117	146	156	176
30	190	114	143	152	171
35	185	111	139	148	167
40	180	108	135	144	162
45	175	105	131	140	158
50	170	102	128	136	153
55	165	99	124	132	149
60	160	96	120	128	144
65	155	93	116	124	140
70	150	90	113	120	135

Diagram 18: Training pulse rate

7.2 Walking Programme for Beginners

If you have given yourself a "4" for your Walking test then this plan is the right one for you.

The given training pulse rate takes into account a performance level rather below average, and the fact that you first need to get used to Walking.

Do not forget to warm-up each time you do your Walking training.

Week	1 - 8	9 - 16	17 - 24	25 - 32	33
Trainings pulse rate (% of maximum pulse)	60%	60%	75%	80%	Walking test
Training time per unit (minutes)	15 – 30	30 – 45	45 – 60	60	Walking test
Units per week	1	2	2-3	3-4	Walking test

Diagram 19: Walking training plan for beginners

Watch out for any initial signs of running out of breath or tightness in your chest.

If such symptoms occur you should stop training immediately and seek a doctor's advice.

Weeks 1-8

During the first eight weeks Walk with a pulse rate of 60% of your maximum 220 pulse minus your age in order to adjust your heart and circulatory system gently to the increased load. The tendons and ligaments are then carefully and correctly exercised.

If you train for no longer than 30 minutes at a time you will ensure that you do not overstrain yourself and maybe spoil your desire to Walk. Keep an eye on your Walking technique.

Weeks 9-16

The next eight weeks serve to stabililise any adjustment problems met so far. As you then increase the length of your Walking training units keep a regular pulse rate, so that later on around week 12 you can Walk up to twice a week.

That is a considerable task during which you should not walk any faster, even if you feel you probably could do.

Only in later weeks can you increase your Walking speed.

Weeks 17-24

In the next 8-week phase of the programme you can start to increase your Walking speed and at the same time also increase your pulse rate to 75% of the maximum pulse (see chart on page 73). This corresponds with the lower limit of continual strain in endurance sport recommended by sports medics.

You will discover that if you exert yourself to this level you have an ideal balance of oxygen intake to oxygen expenditure (steady state), and thus overcharging the system is virtually impossible. At the end of this phase of training you should increase your range of training to three Walking hours per week.

Weeks 25-32

This time you can increase your Walking tempo with a range of training of 4 x 60 minutes until you reach the upper limit of a training pulse of 80% maximum for your age as you Walk, which is recommended by the sports medics. This is the best way of increasing your endurance performance potential in a gentle and careful way. You have already long since noticed how your body has adapted to all this, for example with a lower pulse rate when at rest, or that you have a lower pulse rate but a higher Walking speed.

Week 33

At this stage you should do the Walking test again. There is a 100% likelihood, when you get your improved test result, that you will see you can Walk faster and do not feel so worn out. This should motivate you to carry on. See if you can now manage the **Walking programme for advanced Walkers.** The ongoing increase in performance is included in the programme.

7.3   Walking Programme for Advanced Walkers

If you have got a "2" or "3" for the Walking test then this next Walking training plan is the right one for you.

Week	1 - 8	9 - 16	17 - 24	25 - 32	33
Training pulse frequency (% of maximum pulse rate)	60 – 75%	60 – 75%	75%	80%	Walking test
Training time per unit (minutes)	30 – 45	45	45 – 60	60	Walking test
Units per week	2	3	3 - 4	4	Walking test

Diagram 20: Walking training plan for advanced Walkers

Weeks 1-8

Train twice a week. Your training pulse should not reach 75% of its maximum (see chart on page 73) until the end of week 7. Try and Walk at this speed for 45 minutes in Week 8.

Optimise your Walking technique during this time and you will then stabilise your average endurance performance potential reached in the Walking test, which you can then increase in the next stages.

Weeks 9-16

At this stage increase the length and frequency of your Walking training. Walk at a speed whereby you can maintain a maximum pulse rate of 75%.

Weeks 17-24

Once again you are now going to increase the range of training in your Walking programme. First of all, raise it to 60 minutes each time so that you can then manage to train four times a week.

Only walk as much as keeps you at the lower continuous performance limit of 75%.

Weeks 25-32

Your by now well-established endurance performance potential is now increased by raising your Walking speed.

You must check that you are not Walking too fast by taking your pulse, and 80% of the maximum pulse rate is quite enough.

Week 33

In the 33rd week you can see whether your fitness level has improved. We expect that it has and that you can now manage excellent long-term performance, so you should consider whether you would like to embark on the **Walking training plan for experts.**

If you follow this programme it is quite possible to quickly improve your performance still further.

7.4 Walking Programme for Experts

Walking for experts is the name given to the training plan for those whose level of performance is above average. If you have got a "1" in the Walking test this is for you. This Walking training plan also works in line with the principle **"Start gently, increase slowly"**.

Before you set off at full throttle you need to feel comfortable with the Walking technique, and you should give yourself plenty of time for this – the first eight weeks.

Week	1 - 8	9 - 16	17 - 24	25 - 32	33
Training pulse frequency (% of maximum pulse rate)	60 – 75%	75%	75–80%	80%	Walking test
Training time per unit (minutes)	30 – 45	45 – 60	60 – 90	90 – 120	Walking test
Units per week	2 – 3	3 – 4	4	4 – 7	Walking test

Diagram 21: Walking training plan for experts

Weeks 1-8

Do not walk any faster than you can probably manage at this stage, because you need to wait for your body to adjust and catch up.

Your endurance level is very good but tendons and ligaments need more time. Settle for a moderate Walking speed in order to polish your Walking technique, because this must be just right if you want to Walk at your maximum speed later.

Weeks 9-16

At this stage increase your range of training without reaching the continuous performance level of 80%. You will manage that in your 17th week when you try to Walk for up to 90 minutes at continous performance speed.

Weeks 17-24

90 minutes of Power Walking at a lower speed than your absolute maximum. You are fit and feel as if you could fell some trees! But we have not finished yet.

Weeks 25-32

Walk with your pulse rate at 90% of its maximum in order to push the aerobic limit, your long-term performance limit, back a bit. Thus you will increase your endurance performance potential again. You are now so fit that you can Walk with power for up to 120 minutes.

Week 33

Using the Walking test on page 53 check whether your Walking speed and test pulse have improved at all. If you are even faster with a lower pulse rate than in your first Walking test then you can hardly improve your endurance performance potential as far as your health is concerned. See that you have enough rests because you surely know that regeneration and load must be balanced against each other. Therefore do not ever Walk over a long period beyond the 80% limit of your pulse rate. The 90% limit only serves to give your body new incentives and to attain greater adaptability.

7.5   Walking Programme for Older People (over 70)

The Walking programme for older people is suited to the over 70s, the generation of the so-called "third age-group", experienced and supple, who want to enjoy the evening of their life.

Walking is the ideal endurance sport for this group of people. Mobility, vitality, general well-being and health are effectively maintained and improved by regular Walking, and also one's quality of life is improved. People learn to trust the strengths of their ageing body and can look to the future more optimistically. The aim is to become fit and more competent, and stay that way to a ripe old age. Moderate Walking movement keeps your heart and circulation fit and active, and your whole metabolism is activated and brought to life. During gentle exertion your brain has just the right blood flow and your blood pressure stays at the correct level.

The whole mobility system, muscles and bones, is strengthened. The danger of osteoporosis and life-threatening falls is minimised because the nerve and muscle processes are continually in demand and thereby maintained.

Older people can fit in with the Walking programme for beginners/see page 73). The Walking programme for the elderly has been modified somewhat:

Week	1 - 8	9 - 16	17 - 24	25 - 32	33 - 40
Training pulse frequency (% of maximum pulse rate)	60%	60%	75%	80%	80%
Training time per unit (minutes)	15	15 – 30	30 – 45	45 – 60	45 – 60
Units per week	1	2	2 - 3	3 - 4	5 - 7

Diagram 22: Programme summary - Walking for the elderly

Your aim should be to Walk for 45-60 minutes per day with a pulse rate of 80% of your maximum 220 minus your age (see chart on page 80). The length of time you go Walking is then about the same as a longer daily walk in the fresh air.

An 80 year-old should Walk with a pulse rate of about 112 per minute. The given pulse rates should serve as a guideline. It is important that you should train with more than ten pulse beats above your normal resting pulse, no matter which training week you are in.

For example, when your pulse rate standing still is 80 then you should train with it at least 90, thus achieving the right result without over-exerting yourself.

age	Maximum pulse rate	Training pulse rate		
	100%	60%	75%	80%
70	150	90	113	120
75	145	87	109	116
80	140	84	105	112
85	135	81	101	108
90	130	78	97	104

(% of 220 minus age)

Diagram 23: Training pulse rate for the elderly

Do not overdo it. These pulse rates are only guidelines. At your age individual fitness is the important factor as fitness and health levels amongst the elderly can vary enormously, even when people are the same age.

Whilst some people feel as if they could pull trees up with their roots, like a 30 year-old, others really feel their age. You are not concerned with winning a medal but rather with your all-round sense of well-being.

It is much nicer if you can go out Walking together with friends as it is more fun in a group. You can chat, make contact with others and cement friendships. Then, once you have finished Walking, you can go for a drink together and enjoy each other's company.

7.6 A Walking Programme for Losing Weight

Walking is the kind of endurance sport where you train within the right sort of pulse rate area for using up deposits of fat inherent in your body.

For people who are overweight and wish to lose some weight or get it under control, Walking is preferable to many other kinds of endurance sport as it takes care of your joints. Unlike when jogging the greater weight does not have to be supported with a lot of effort and pressure on the joints.

Training intensity zone (% of maximum heart rate)	Maximum heart rate										
	150	155	160	165	170	175	180	185	190	195	200
Fat-burning zone (50%-60%)	75 to 90	78 to 93	80 to 96	83 to 99	85 to 102	88 to 105	90 to 108	93 to 111	95 to 114	98 to 117	100 to 120

Diagram 24: Fat combustion areas

Frequent Walking does you more good than any diet. Even if you find losing weight difficult the proportion of fat to amount of muscle changes in your favour. The best sort of combination for guaranteed weight reduction is a calorie-reduced diet and a moderate, gently strenuous kind of endurance exercise like Walking.

The advantage compared with a diet where no movement is involved is that the calorie-burning muscles do not change their composition at all, but are primarily rather more concerned with getting rid of unwanted fat.

While you are Walking your whole organism uses up energy in the form of carbohydrates and fats already stored away in the body. The metabolic rate, i.e. the using up of these energy substances in the muscles, is increased by Walking. Thus, you make much better use of your food than if you only diet.

Look at the pulse rates for the fat combustion areas (see diagram 42) for your Walking training. Walk the right amount for your age and in the given pulse rate areas, because Walking stimulates your fat metabolic rate to work at its maximum level with the minimum amount of exertion, so that you always have enough energy at your disposal for Walking.

It is important and ideal for you to Walk for at least 60 minutes, because then between 50 and 70% of your body's required energy is attained by getting rid of body fat. If you have any of the usual side-effects of overweight e.g. raised blood pressure or joint problems, then you should consult your doctor before you embark on this Walking programme.

Week	1 – 8	9 – 16	17 – 24	25 – 32
Training pulse frequency (% of maximum pulse- rate)	60%	60%	75%	80%
Training time per unit (minutes)	15	15 – 30	45	60
Units per week	4	4	5	7

Diagram 25: Programme survey – losing weight by Walking

Weeks 1-8

At this stage of the programme it is important that you first reduce weight, and secondly that you start Walking slowly so that your foot, knee and hip joints get used to the load put upon them.

Therefore, Walk four times a week for about 15 minutes, whilst accompanying your programme with low-calorie food.

Weeks 9-16

During the following eight weeks you can increase your Walking time within the same range to 30 minutes per Walking session, and you will find that your fat metabolic rate is set well in motion. Keep up your low-calorie diet.

Weeks 17-24

Now you can increase your range of training considerably by Walking for 45 minutes five times a week.

Your body will only manage this by setting to work on the fat deposits. You will probably already lose weight during this stage i.e. your skin will become firm and parts of your body toned up.

Now we are really getting somewhere! Walk for at least 60 minutes a day, that means work at and get rid of some calories every day. That also means: loss of weight! A low-calorie diet helps you lose weight when you Walk, but it is often hard to stop eating your favourite foods.

The clue lies in noticing where and when you like eating, because your will is often inclined to get you to eat differently. Without realising you often return to certain kinds of food.

If you find it hard to alter your eating habits we recommend some recognised courses for dieting. These are an ideal supplement to our Walking programme for losing weight.

8. Walking with ...

Walking (as a sporting activity) is happily made use of in a therapeutic manner for certain illnesses. The following sections give a brief summary of when it is all right to Walk as mobility therapy after an appropriate patient-doctor interview.

8.1 ... Back Problems or Injury to Your Mobility System

Walking is the kind of sport which produces up to three times less of a shock load on the body than slow running. But it is suggested that one Walks before embarking on running training in order to build-up one's old performance potential slowly.

For almost all sporting injuries Walking can maintain one's training condition and indeed, after a lengthy break due to injury, can help restore the original performance level very quickly.

Walking is suitable as mobility training for people who have signs of wear and tear to their foot, knee, hip joints and their spine and must avoid any kind of sudden jolt which could injure such joints or the spine.

Walking is a good thing here in that it trains endurance ability as well as bringing about the same sort of results as running and jogging.

Since the end of the 60s one knows that physical inactivity can lead to a deterioration of ailments like arthritis (inflamed overworked joint), just one of a number of similar conditions. Innovative sport medics have been successfully marketing the idea for years that a moderate amount of sport halts or slows down these processes. Walking is just such a moderate sporting activity.

8.2 ... Certain Illnesses

With certain prerequisites, Walking as therapy (after an injury or illness) and as rehabilitation (getting moving again after serious illness) is the best thing you can do. Indeed for certain types of illness therapeutic Walking works well alongside traditional kinds of therapy e.g. at certain stages of osteoporosis, certain injuries, or wear and tear on one's mobility system, or if suffering from heart disease. It is not possible here to offer a fixed Walking programme for every kind of illness. Each individual patient must proceed according to their performance potential and state of health at the time, which is only possible in collaboration with one's doctor and mobility therapist.

8.2.1   ... Osteoporosis
Osteoporosis usually afflicts middle-aged people, and is a reduction of bone material, although the bone itself does not change its shape. After all growth is complete (after the age of 35), there is a perfectly normal ageing process of the bones set against an impaired rebuilding of the bones. This can be seen much more clearly in women than in men, due to the reduced hormone production in and during the menopause.

Usual symptoms of osteoporosis are pain occurring in the back and lower spinal column, which can be triggered off by hair-line cracks in the vertebrae. You can ward off the disease by Walking and a calcium-rich diet.

Walking as mobility therapy is well-suited to reducing the symptoms and preventing further development of the disease in its early stages. The incentive to move which Walking gives, improves the bones' metabolism.

Walking is also ideal because any pressure on other joints is much less than in other endurance sports, and you can do it anywhere. If you are afflicted with osteoporosis ask your doctor whether it is all right to Walk, because in later stages of the disease you are only allowed a special kind of osteoporosis gymnastics.

8.2.2   ... Angina Pectoris
For certain groups of people with heart problems Walking is just the thing for therapeutic Walking training, and is also of interest as endurance training for so-called heart-sport groups.

Walking as mobility therapy must be carefully measured and kept under control. A desirable side-effect of Walking is that it has a positive influence on the risk factors of arterial sclerosis in the body's extremities, like an improvement in one's fat metabolism and the speed of one's blood flow.

But you must get your doctor's consent, and if you fall into the risk category find out if it is all right to Walk at all.

8.2.3 ... Vein Problems e.g. Varicose Veins

Walking is the best possible preventative treatment for vein problems even if you already suffer. Then, what could be better than Walking for getting the legs' muscle pumps going in a gentle and protective way and activating your circulation at the same time?

In your legs you have a superficial (epifascial) and deep (subfascial) vein system. The deep vein system lies between you muscles and tendons.

The superficial vein system lies above your muscles and is surrounded by subcutaneous fat connecting tissues and skin. Both vein systems are connected to each other by arteries.

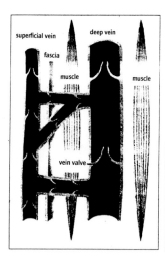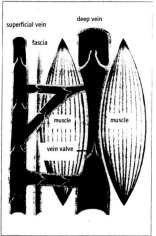

Diagram 26: Vein system

The blood is sucked from the superficial veins through to the deeper vein system, so that this does not overflow, and the blood can then flow into the main vein through your loins and on into your pelvic veins back to your heart.

Vein problems are changes in the deep and superficial vein system. In the superficial vein system they manifest themselves as little twiglets (i.e. mini varicose veins), reticular varicose veins (larger sagging) and varicose veins. The blood flow is disturbed by the sagging veins, and the blood can shoot up to the surface from the deeper veins and cause an ulcer or swelling in the artery. This can cause inflamed veins or blood clots.

In the deeper vein system a blood clot can lead to a thrombosis and block the flow of blood back to the heart. If this thrombosis is not treated in time the vein valves become damaged, the valve function is disturbed, which can lead to a so-called post-thrombosis syndrome i.e. the blood is no longer carried away effectively and gets clogged up. More and more tissue fluid is pushed out of the vessels and this can lead to an open leg wound (ulcer cruris).

At the very worst a blood clot finds its way into the lungs; if there is a blockage there, causing a lung embolism, the original vein problems can have fatal consequences!

The first signs of a vein problem are tired and heavy legs, also an uneasy feeling or hot feet often indicate the same problem. If you get cramps in your calves in the night, your feet swell or even your ankles or legs, then the vein problem is at an advanced stage. You should certainly consult a doctor if you have pain in your legs.

If a superficial vein hurts and is red then an inflammation called phlebitis is the problem. Swollen legs which are a reddish blue and sensitive to pressure indicate thrombosis in the deeper vein system.

Walking strengthens the leg muscles and tightens the connecting tissue and thus the working of the calves' muscle pump is improved, important for taking used blood back towards the heart. Each step that you Walk, because of the muscle movement in calf and thigh, causes alternating pressure on the veins running deep below the surface.

If the muscles contract they force the blood as in a sponge out of the deep veins into the superficial transporting veins. The vein valves prevent the blood flowing back again when the muscle relaxes.

Rhythmic Walking pumps the used blood back in the best possible way and the legs are freed of blockages.

Walking is not only important for the return flow of blood to the heart, but also for keeping the veins in a healthy and elastic state. Even if you have hereditary vein weakness, regular Walking prevents or delays vein problems in many cases.

9   Your Diet and Walking

Eating the right foods is a topic which has not only increased in importance for athletes in recent years. Not only is our diet important for our general fitness but a cornerstone for our health. However, in the following section we only want to take a brief look at this wide-ranging topic and give you a few tips for Walking and nutrition.

9.1   The Importance of a Correct Diet for Our Health

The enormous range of food available in the shops does not exactly simplify our sensible selection of food products. In spite of the wide variety, food consists primarily of three chemically definable components:

- Carbohydrates
- Fats, and
- Proteins.

These principle components of our nutrition are supplemented by vitamins, minerals and trace elements, vital to our well-being.

By means of your body's metabolism your cells can digest the food they receive and immediately turn the dissolved matter into energy or keep it in stock for other occasions when food is scarce.

Normally your body burns up carbohydrates and fats at a steady rate. Proteins do not carry any significant amount of energy but aid the enzyme chain during metabolism. If we do not get the right balance in our diet by eating too much fat and sugar and not enough roughage then we are in trouble.

Put a wrong diet together with too little movement and you run the risk of putting on weight. Of course, our body is capable of tolerating an imbalanced diet for a while, but at some point it will run out of patience.

9.2   What and how much Can We Eat?

You must make sure that you have enough wholefoods in your diet. As a Walking athlete these foods must be in the right ratio to each other, with the bulk being carbohydrate and the rest proteins and fats.

Amount in %	Nutritional product	Means of nutrition
approx. 15-25%	Protein	e.g. milk, yoghurt, cheese, lean meat
approx. 15-25%	Fat	e.g. milk, yoghurt, cheese
approx. 60%	Carbohydrate	e.g. cereal products, potatoes, noodles, fruit

Diagram 27: Chart of nutritional intake as a %

9.3   Walking and Drinking

When you Walk you have a greater loss of salt and minerals and salt is vital for the body's water supply. Minerals are necessary for vital body functions, and vitamins have various roles in our metabolic processes and the digestion of our foods.

So, make sure you get enough of all these subsidiary products.

- Avoid fat i. e. fatty products.
- Avoid sugar i.e. sweet foods.
- Reduce your alcohol intake.
- Replace white flour products with wholemeal ones.
- Eat five small meals per day.
- Drink at least 1,5-2 litres per day and considerably more if you are involved in physical exercise.

Diagram 28: six tips for a well-balanced diet

If you follows the above tips carefully they will help you consciously to change your diet in the longer term.

This will support your performance progress when Walking, when you are aware that foods, which are easy to digest with minimum expenditure of energy, make your body perform better.

10. Tips for the Walking Expert

The following tips are aimed at the high performers amongst Walkers. Power-Walkers can structure their training as they wish in various ways. We will now show you some of these types of "game".

10.1 Walking training with extra Weights

Walking experts can increase their load intensity by using weights (little dumb-bells or weight bands in their hands or round their lower arm).

In this way you can demand more effort from your trunk, shoulder and arm muscles and so train them better. The load stimulus is considerably greater and thus the body's exhaustion factor greater.

Photo 19: Dumb-bells, weight bands

Walking training with dumb-bells should only be done by experienced Walkers.

10.2. Walking Training over Difficult Terrain (Hill Walking)

As the name suggests, Hill Walking involves going uphill. Compared with mountaineering the sporting aspect predominates as the attempt is made to keep up the Walking tempo on a hill. During the ascent Hill

Walkers will have a similar heartbeat rate to high-performance marathon Walkers, so it is important here to train within the heartbeat areas proven to be health-promoting.

So, you should only go Hill Walking if your health and performance standard permit.

Photo 20: Day-pack

A TIP:

When coming downhill during Hill Walking you place great strain on your joints and spinal column, and therefore, as far as planning the amount of load is concerned, you should put the main emphasis of your training on the ascent, and take great care to go slowly during the descent.

Also, remember that your muscles are tired and your movements not as well co-ordinated, which means you run the risk of injury to your upper and lower ankle-joints. Your muscles are stretched 20 times more when coming down a hill than when going up!

Now vary your training so that you try out different surfaces.

Before you attempt any great inclines you should have done some training in hilly country with flat areas, so that you are better prepared for increased performance and protected against unpleasant surprises.

10.3 Body Walking (Meditative Walking)

The development of the human spirit starts with physical experiences, which then ultimately lead towards intellectual or spiritual development. So, Body Walking is suitable for anyone who wishes to get through to their innermost self via their body, and this by means of meditation and relaxation.

The Body Walking movements are rhythmic and harmonious, seeming to have neither beginning nor end. They intertwine and unravel themselves again, so that Body Walking gives you the feeling that body and spirit are in tune with each other. At some point your spirit will drive your Walking, steered by the flow of energy from your breathing. Body Walking is meditation and relaxation by means of your body, where your body is the means by which you see yourself and your surroundings in a new light.

It is important that you find your own Body Walking rhythm. The following effects of Body Walking stem from a watchful observance of your body:

- Find an area which is quiet and peaceful. Car and traffic noise should be avoided. Prepare yourself for Body Walking by concentrating.
- Take up a firm and restful position where your body weight flows into your feet, and thus you will stand firm, like a tree rooted into the ground. Feel the strength coming out of the ground into your feet. Think yourself into Body Walking by imagining the gently flowing, harmonious Walking movement.
- Walk slowly to start with, remaining upright and comfortable, with a relaxed body. You will feel light and mobile, and your spirit is quiet as you concentrate on the Body Walking. Increase your speed to a pleasantly moderate level of exertion.
- Body Walking is closely connected with your breathing. Be aware of how life-giving energy flows into your body, is collected and dispersed to every part of your body. Breathing out mobilises your life-giving energy. You open up and cleanse your innermost being, and thus, naturally, take deeper breaths.
- It is possible to get rid of muscular tension by breathing. Guide your breathing into the part of your body which feels tense i.e. breathe into your "arm" or your "stomach". Feel how fresh energy is released, which frees blocked-up energy so that life-giving energy flows through your body again.

- Your Walking movements and your spirit become one. You Walk more freely and without being cramped, and your Walking movements come from the middle of your body, pelvis and hips to form the foundation. Arms and legs move in a free, even and harmonious ensemble.

- Now concentrate on the rhythmic Walking movement and you will feel how a pleasant heaviness spreads out through your limbs and on into your feet, so that you feel the ground. You then get the feeling that new energy is coming up towards you. Weather and ground permitting you can go barefoot, but the best sort of ground is soft but firm sand, or the springy floor of a forest.

- At some point you will become one with your surroundings. Your senses are alert in all directions, inwards as well as outwards. The environment pours into you with every breath you take. You really feel the completeness and uniformity of everything around you. Let every impression really sink into you and sense the living environment in every fibre of your being. You will receive a cleansing sensation, being part of a wonderful, universal whole. Suddenly you know that you are connected and infused with everything. Unexpected security and relaxation flows through you and you feel like a drop of water hidden in the river of life. Past, present and future melt into one; you live in the here and now and are led along by your Body Walking.

- Taste this moment of happiness to the full, as in it, this tiny moment you experience the world just as it is for you. Body Walking is a sensuous experience of the world as a complete whole, and your body is the means of experiencing it.

- At the end of your Body Walking practice time you can actively return from this state of immersion into yourself. Be consciously aware of your return and then you are relaxed, clear-headed and calm to face what lies before you, not tired or dizzy. Do not bother about this return procedure if you intend going straight to bed.

- Reduce your Walking tempo slowly until you finally stop. Assume again the firm and restful position you had to start with. The weight of your body sinks into your feet.

- Now clench your fists, stretch out your arms and pull them energetically towards your body. Then breathe in and out deeply several times, so that you can hear yourself clearly. Loosen up all your limbs and have a good look round with your eyes wide open.

Do your Body Walking as often as possible, giving yourself plenty of time. It takes a while to get used to concentrating on your body and achieving an awareness of it. The various effects described here do not necessarily happen immediately. What is important is that you Walk regularly without setting any time limit.

Untrained people will need to Walk longer initially to reach the right meditative state.

11   Tips and Tricks from Olympic Medallist in Race Walking - Hartwig Gauder

Warming-up

During warming-up, muscles previously still cold are brought up to working temperature and prepared for the approaching effort (stretching). The blood vessels open up slowly, and the body finds time to adjust to the impending exercise.

You can concentrate better and also improve your motor responses for Walking. Quietly and without any stress prepare your mind for the sporting exercise to come. Warming-up should begin with gymnastics on the spot, and finally end with some specialised Walking gymnastics once all the moving is over.

Clothing

Depending on the time of year you should equip yourself with various combinations. A classical tracksuit is always a good idea, but close-fitting tights are the most practical. For cold, windy and rainy weather you need a mixture of a weather protective outer garment and air-tex underwear.

The weather protective garment should be water-resistant, light-weight material with air holes, giving ventilation to the under-garments. This clothing must be windproof, so that your body does not lose heat whilst Walking. The underwear must be capable of channelling sweat from your body to the outside.

Characteristics of endurance

My level of endurance pleases me in that I am now capable of managing not only at least 50 kilometres on foot, but also of carrying out many things in my everyday life more reliably and with better concentration.

However, the basic requirements for endurance training remain good health and as good an actual awareness as possible of your performance potential at the time.

Diet

People who eat in a balanced way and get enough exercise do not need any special diet. Obviously in competitions like the Olympic Games, or International Championships, I had my own special kind of diet, but I do not wish to make any generalizations for improving your performance. Contrary to many ideas as to how we athletes feed ourselves my basic diet was not just salads and muesli. My motto is in "variable and varied".

A healthy mixed diet of vegetables, fruit, cereals, milk products, salads, fish or lean meat is the best. You should constantly try out what you like and what likes you. A cosy feeling in your tummy is more important than many tips.

Eating before Walking

The same rules apply here as when practising any kind of sport. The guiding principle is that you should Walk on neither an empty nor a full stomach. Small meals spread over the course of a day are better than three large meals. A main meal can be consumed three or four hours prior to Walking.

There is no objection to a small energy snack 40-60 minutes beforehand, a cup of tea or a glass of fruit juice.

Feet

It is a kind of paradox that our feet are given the most wear and tear, but as far as looking after them is concerned, we treat them like a stepmother! They would be grateful for better treatment e.g.: we often force our feet into fashionable shoes, which are too tight, rather than giving them the same treatment which our hands usually get i.e. rub cream into your feet after a tiring day; treat yourself to an occasional foot massage or a warm footbath.

Also, if you roll the soles of your feet over a round bit of wood it will give you a pleasant, relaxed feeling.

Health

Health is not something which we always have inside us, but rather a lifelong process which we can influence ourselves. Even after completing over 120.000 kilometres on foot, I cannot say that I have done enough for myself with that. Even I operate according to the maxim: "Get mobile by Walking and stay mobile."

If you practise active Walking you will soon discover that you can increase your immunity to disease, improve your spiritual well-being and maintain an active lifestyle; that is if you adapt your Walking training to your level of fitness do it regularly and aim to relax at the same time.

Help with massaging parts of the body

- Head massage   ➝   Use your fingertips.
- Shoulder massage ➝ Swing your arms to loosen up, then knead and stroke.

- Upper and lower arm massage ➝ Stroke outwards and knead.
- Hands   ➝   Stroke outwards, knead and give them a good shake.

- Lower back   ➝   Rub the lumbar vertebrae.
- Bottom   ➝   surface massage.
- Tummy   ➝   Stroke in a clockwise direction
- Thighs   ➝   Knead, stroke outwards, surface message
- Shins   ➝   Knead, stroke outwards, shake your calves.
- Shins muscles   ➝   Stroke outwards with the ball of your hands.
- Feet   ➝   Stroke outwards, knead the outer edges.

Intensity

The amount of load which I feel personally is still my main criterion during sporting exercise, in spite of all the recently-introduced technical aids.

I can only accurately assess my performance capacity on any particular day and minimise disturbance factors if I have the right kind of feeling towards my body.

If in any doubt each fit Walker should apply the principle: "Settle for Walking a bit slower, even if it takes you a few minutes more time."

Jogging

The Jogging movement has already been superseded by Walking in the U.S.A. In a quick and uncomplicated way the Americans have soon recognised the healthy aspects of Walking.

But whoever feels inadequately stretched by Walking should give way to his feelings and apply the motto: "Reach jogging by Walking".

Performance Test

The results of performance tests give the prerequisite for the derivation of load recommendations. Possible test results could be:

- A test protocol
- An estimation of performance
- A recommendation for mobility training
- A recommendation for further exercise
- A means of controlling one's training and guiding it.

People

Most people are sociable by nature, so it is a good idea if you intend starting Walking to ask some of your friends if they would like to Walk with you. Many people are looking for just such an opportunity and you will notice it is more fun in a group, especially as there is always plenty of space for a good chat.

Foods

Carbohydrates were always my main source of energy and I got my protein in a combination of plant and animal proteins in addition to my normal diet. I have tried to avoid fat because there is a high percentage of fat in one's normal diet. If you eat a balanced diet you get enough vitamins. Minerals are mainly shed in sweat, but can be replaced quickly by drinking fizzy apple juice after your Walking.

Olympics

Sportive Walking (Race Walking), practised as a competitive sport, is one of the oldest disciplines in the Olympic Games. During the Olympics the 20 kilometre and the 50 kilometre Walk for men, and the 10 kilometre Walk for women, are contested as racing routes. The top Walkers reach an average speed of about 13.68 kilometres per hour over the 50 kilometre route.

Pulse

The pulse or heartbeat rate is one of the easiest ways in which we gauge our stress level. The easiest way of finding this out is to take one's pulse at the wrist or main neck artery for 15 seconds and multiply by 4 to get the pulse rate per minute. One usually uses the middle and ring-finger on the appropriate artery, but this method unfortunately carries a high error factor e.g.

- People do not start counting their pulse as soon as they stop Walking
- People miscount, because the pulse rate is too high.
- They do not find the right artery fast enough.

And there is another disadvantage: the pulse rate cannot be taken during exercise, which is the time when it is needed more than when one has finished Walking. So, manual pulse rate readings are only a rough guide, and therefore we recommend a pulse watch (available in specialist shops and all sports shops).

But, be careful: my experience has shown that not all pulse watches are what they are cracked up to be!

Regeneration

You recover fast from the pleasant tiredness following a dose of Walking training. After you have quenched your thirst and had a shower you will feel a lot better than before exercising. An important tip straight after training: "Get those sweaty clothes off!" because of the risk of catching a cold. Should you find however that the training was a bit too taxing or too intensive for that particular day, then your body and spirit will need some extra care.

Give yourself a brush massage (with a soft and flexible natural brush from your toes to your head), or an alternating warm-cold shower (starting warm and finishing cold) to help you to relax and stimulate your circulatory system.

Aching calves

Calf muscles can well cause Walking beginners a certain amount of pain. Please do not panic if this happens to you. Stand still for a minute and stroke your calf muscles with the ball of your hands. A bit of foot-rolling can also ease the pain.

If you belong to the sort of Walkers who suffer from calf muscle pain then look for soft ground when you warm up and get rid of the tension after Walking with alternating baths. In our experience these pains disappear after a few hours of practice.

Type of training

As a beginner you should exercise according to the "endurance method", though without any undue strain to yourself. That means Walking for about 45 minutes at an even tempo, ensuring that you aim rather to extend your Walking time or route than to increase your speed.

If you feel more of an expert after a few weeks and have had your progress confirmed by the Walking test, then it is essential to work to a Walking training programme made specially for you, to become even fitter in the future.

The guiding principle of this programme should be to vary your training, because if you do not and, as an experienced Walker, continually walk the same route within the same time span, then you will never see any improvement because your body is not receiving enough of an incentive or the need to adapt further. As a result you will not be able to keep renewing your performance standard and you could possibly lose your enjoyment of Walking.

Accidents
Unfortunately sport accidents can occur even if one is taking adequate care. Should an accident occur it is important to proceed correctly at the scene of the accident. With all the usual sporting injuries like bruising, sprains, straining or pulled ligaments, one should first try and prevent swelling and bleeding.

We recommend an immediate compress (failing all else with one's hand) and cooling treatment. Only a doctor can make an accurate diagnosis and set the right sort of therapy in motion. If you follow the above suggestions you will aid the doctor's healing work considerably.

By just putting a bit of ointment on the wound you are setting the scene maybe for a worse injury.

A long bath
A nice long bath, with or without any bath oils etc., is an ideal kind of relaxation after strenuous Walking. The temperature should not exceed 40°C (about 102°F) but ideally be between 37°C and 39°C (98-100°F): you should spend between ten and twenty minutes in the bath.

Walking technique
It is important to know that there is no ideal Walking technique which you can see just by watching the gait of any person.

Everyone has their own individual style and Walking is no exception. All the previously described Walking techniques serve merely to help you optimise your own method of locomotion and eliminate errors so that everyone can enjoy Walking, playfully improve one's fitness, sweat off everyday frustrations properly and enjoy physical exhaustion.

Last but not least
It is never too late to start Walking.

If all your personal prerequisites, opportunities and aims are in tune with each other, then you will achieve maximum success. There is no difference between a professional and a leisure athlete.

Eradicate the words "I have no time for Walking" from your vocabulary and take time, which you will find personally beneficial.

On to the next Walking meeting; perhaps we will meet there some day.

Have a good Walk,
Yours, *Hartwig Gauder*

12   Appendix

12.1   Helpful Addresses

The following institutions will give you information about Walking courses or Walking meetings in your area:

- Health insurance organisations
- Further education colleges

Information about instruments for measuring your heartbeat is available from:

Polar Electro GmbH Deutschland
Postfach 154
64570 Büttelborn

Polar Electro oy
Professorintie 5
SF 90440 Kempele

12.4   List of Diagrams/Photos

References

diagram 1:   Bös/Renzland: Sport, Spiel, Spaß.
                In: Johann-Wolfgang-Goethe-Universität Frankfurt
                (Hrsg.): Forschung Frankfurt, Frankfurt 1989.

photo 7:   Polar Electro GmbH Deutschland, Büttelborn

diagram 12:   Geiger, C., Ausdauersport-Leitfaden,
                Oberhaching 1988.

diagram 24:   Sally Edwards, Leitfaden zur Trainingskontrolle,
                Aachen 1993.

diagram 26:   out of „Venen-Walking", with kind permission of
                Intersan GmbH, Ettlingen

photo 19:   Polar Electro GmbH Deutschland, Büttelborn

photo 20:   Polar Electro GmbH Deutschland, Büttelborn

any further diagrams and photos: Klaus Bös, Frankfurt

Our Scientific Programme

- Sport Sciences in Europe 1993 – Current and Future Perspectives
- Physical Education and Sport –Changes and Challenges
- Racism and Xenophobia in European Football
- The Chelsea School Research Centre Edition Volumes 1-7

  - Biomechanical Research Project
  - Physical Activity for Life: East and West, South and North
  - Cultural Diversity and Congruence in PE and Sport
  - Physical Education: A Reader
  - Integration through Games and Sports
  - Recreational Games and Tournaments

MEYER & MEYER • SPORT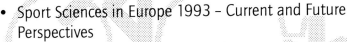

Internet: http://www.meyer-meyer-sports.com
e-mail: verlag@meyer-meyer-sports.com

- Handbook for Beach Volleyball
- Volleyball – A Handbook for Coaches and Players
- Allround Fitness
- Jazz Dance Training
- Contact Improvisation
- Teaching Children's Gymnastics
- Train your Brain

  - Adventure Sports – Big Foot
  - Mountainbike Training
  - The Complete Guide to Duathlon Training
  - The Complete Guide to Triathlon Training
  - Handbook of Competitive Cycling
  - Modern Sports Karate
  - Scientific Coaching for Olympic Taekwondo

MEYER & MEYER • SPORT N

Internet: http://www. meyer-meyer-sports.com
e-mail: verlag@ meyer-meyer-sports.com

ur English Programme

- Coaching Tips for Children 's Soccer
- Junior Soccer – A Manual for Coaches
- Soccer Training Programmes
- Training Exercises for Competitive Tennis
- Advanced Techniques for Competitive Tennis
- Straight Golf

- Running to the Top
- Distance Training for Young Athletes
- Distance Training for Women Athletes
- Successful Running
- Successful Endurance Training
- Walking
- Nutrition in Sport

MEYER & MEYER • SPORT

Internet: http: //www. meyer-meyer-sports.com
e-mail: verlag@ meyer-meyer-sports.com